MYSTERIOUS DORSET

Rodney Legg

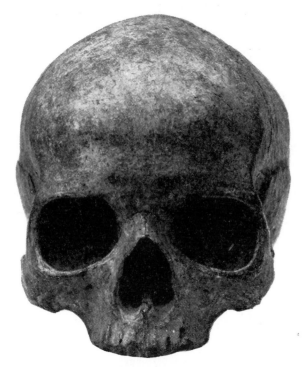

Bettiscombe's 'Screaming Skull': see pages 11-13.

DORSET PUBLISHING COMPANY
NATIONAL SCHOOL, NORTH STREET,
WINCANTON, SOMERSET BA9 9AT

Also by Rodney Legg

Editor and principal contributor *Dorset County Magazine [1968-87]*,
ditto *Dorset 'Explore' Magazine [1995-97]*,
and now *Dorset Country Magazine [from 1998]*

For
Mark Eden
who asked me to
write him some stories

Publishing details. First published 1987. Second impression 1998.
Copyright Rodney Legg © 1987-98.

Printing credits.
Typeset by Santype International Ltd at Salisbury.
Printed in Great Britain by FWB Printing, Southgate Road, Wincanton, Somerset.

Distrubtion. Trade sales distribution by Halsgrove Publishing, Lower Moor Way,
Tiverton, Devon EX16 6SS. Telephone 01-994-243-242

International standard book number (ISBN) 0 948699 65 5

Legend – two killers hanged in chains on what is now the churchyard sundial at Parley: see page 130.

Ghost – Colonel Francis Claridge ebullient at Sandford Orcas manor house: see pages 55-59.

Puzzle – try to figure out this cryptic Christchurch epitaph, before turning to the author's attempt which is on page 103.

WE WERE NOT SLAYNE BVT RAYSD
RAYSD NOT TO LIFE
BVT TO BE BVRIED TWICE
BY MEN OF STRIFE
WHAT REST COVLD TH LIVING HAVE
WHEN DEAD HAD NONE
AGREE AMONGST YOV
HEERE WE TEN ARE ONE
HEN: ROGERS DIED APRILL 17 1641
I R

Ghosts – a grey lady, duellists
and an ape – in a superb Tudor setting
at Athelhampton Hall: see page 4.

Custom – the 'byzant' ceremony
on hilltop Shaftesbury, descending
with the town's offerings for the well-owners
at Enmore Green: see page 120.

While yet a boy I sought for ghosts, and sped
Through many a listening chamber, cave and ruin,
And starlight wood, with fearful steps pursuing
Hope of high talk with the departed dead.

— PERCY BYSSHE SHELLEY [HYMN TO INTELLECTUAL BEAUTY]

GHOSTS

From ghoulies and ghosties and long-leggety beasties
And things that go bump in the night,
Good Lord, deliver us!

— FROM A SCOTTISH PRAYER

Haunted with sadness –
the Manor House at Lytchett Matravers,
since demolished.
See pages 39-42.

Hyperactive with hauntings –
the Manor House at Sandford Orcas.
See pages 55-59.

AFFPUDDLE [hamlet of BRIANTSPUDDLE]

Headless men were carrying a coffin

LOIS WALKER, who from 1921 until 1946 was headmistress of Affpuddle village school, was told by an old lady in the nearby hamlet of Briantspuddle about the day her mother was gathering kindle on the fringe of the heath towards Cullpepper's Dish. She rested on her way home, by the wayside, as she was carrying a large bundle. Then she heard the tramping of feet and saw a coffin being carried down the lane by four headless men.

"The woman fled leaving her sticks behind, and nothing would persuade her to go that way again," Walker writes in *A School among the Puddles*. "I visited the wood many times and there certainly was an air of mystery enshrouding it. Adjoining was a derelict keeper's cottage. On investigation, I was told that no one would live there, keeper after keeper leaving because of strange noises, 'things that go bump in the night', like breaking crockery and overturning of chairs, but the cause could not be discovered. The cottage has now completely disappeared; only a few straggling gooseberry bushes are left among the briars."

ASHMORE

Gabbygammies

TILL ABOUT 1840, there was an ancient burial mound beside the Ashmore to Fontmell Magna cart track by Folly Hanging Gate at Washers Pit [Ordnance Survey map reference ST 898 168]. This solitary place was notorious for the weird sounds of creatures in the air, called Gabbygammies or otherwise Gappergennies. Though the strange sounds could be imitated by human lips, Mr. Stephen Hall of Manor Farm had another explanation and said badgers were the cause. Villagers at Ashmore, however, were sure the place was haunted.

The ghostly noises ceased about 1840 when a metalled road replaced the dusty track; the 4,000-year-old round barrow was removed and the present road passes over its site. Bones dug from the low mound were reburied in Ashmore churchyard. Another oddity of Washers Pit was that countrymen kept a cross of white chalk cut in the turf by the roadside, opposite the barrow, probably to mark the site of a death resulting from an accident or murder. This custom came to an end with the destruction of the burial mound.

Washers Pit was also haunted during the nineteenth century by the ghostly figure of a woman in white who was seen, and felt, brushing by travellers towards Spinneys Pond. There is a story about the cook of a Squire Barber who saved a lady in white who was found hanging, but still alive, from an ash tree over the well, now closed, at Washers Pit about the year of 1700. This incident may have provided the name for Folly Hanging Gate.

Ashmore parish contains some of the remotest lost corners of Cranborne Chase where coombes cut deep into the downland, which rises to eight hundred feet, and before the coming of modern forestry, many clumps of beech were hanging on the steep hillslopes. A narrow unmade lane winds for three miles along the foot of Stubhampton Bottom but passes not a single building. Yet Washers Pit is the one part of Ashmore with a reputation for being haunted, maybe because it alone out of the vast area of deserted chalk uplands, had a small pocket of population from prehistoric times onwards.

ASKERSWELL

Rocks hurled

REV. H. BRYAN was reading in The Times of strange happenings at Swanton Novers, East Anglia, where he once lived, and decided to write from Askerswell Rectory to the editor of the newspaper.

His letter, published on 6 September 1919, recorded that similar poltergeist phenomena took place in his parish of Askerswell, four miles east of Bridport, during the latter half of the nineteenth century when scores of people came from the town to witness the nightly supernatural occurrences. Immense pieces of rock were hurled from one room to another, all supposedly coming from the ceiling. The incidents ceased altogether when an hysterical girl left the house for another, which was soon to be found on fire.

ATHELHAMPTON

Martyn's ape

ATHELHAMPTON HALL, one mile east of Puddletown on the A35 [Ordnance Survey map reference SY 770 943], is an ancient haunted house to which visitors are welcome during the summer. Mr. James Wentworth Day has collected stories of a phantom ape, ghostly duellists, a hooded monk in black, and a cooper who hammers in a cellar on his non-existent wine barrels. Mr. Day also writes of a housemaid, now retired, who walked into the Tudor room at Athelhampton and saw a lady in grey, sitting in a chair just after the day's visitors had gone. On being told the house was closing and that her party had left, the grey lady rose without a word and vanished through the wooden panelling at the base of the wall. Other members of the household staff have also discovered the lady of the Tudor room.

Not nowadays seen is the ghost of a tame monkey, kept by members of the Martyn family who erected the earliest part of the house in the fifteenth century. Their crest was of an ape sitting on a tree stump, and the motto was: "He who looks at Martyn's ape, Martyn's ape will look at him." The legend is that a girl of the Martyn family, who had been jilted in love, opened a secret door in the panelling near a fireplace in the great chamber and went up a staircase to a room where she killed herself. An unfortunate ape followed her, but as it was not seen, she shut the door at the top of the stairs, imprisoning the creature in the staircase where it died of starvation.

Once a guest was relaxing in the great chamber when she looked up and saw two young men come into the room and, without speaking, start to duel. She called on them to stop fighting but was ignored, and no servant came when she rang the bell in despair. The duel continued till one of the men was slashed across the arm and the pair left the room. When later she told the owner she thought he had extraordinary people staying there, he answered: "I can't understand what you are talking about as you met all the guests who are staying here, at tea."

BEAMINSTER

The ghost of a Monmouth rebel

MISS KATHLEEN PIM recalled the ghostly footsteps at Rose Cottage, Beaminster, for Amanda Allsop in 1975. The cottage and its gardens are one of the most cheerful and placid spots in this quiet country town, sandwiched as the splash of colour between the old Tanyard and a range of nineteenth century cottages behind the parish church. Miss Pim was born in Beaminster, the daughter of a doctor, and bought Rose Cottage in 1955.

It was then neglected and dilapidated and the Georgian structure needed major renovation. The builders found a Civil War cannonball in the garden. Miss Pim could not move in until April 1956 and the year was to close with a mystery that would stay on her mind. She was able to recount all the relevant times for Amanda Allsop who takes up the story:

"On 21 December 1956 the night was calm, clear and bright, and in those days the church clock chimed out a hymn every three hours. Miss Pim awoke to the sound of that week's hymn, and at the same time heard the garden gate strain heavily. She assumed that it was the 6 a.m. chime, and that the paper boy had arrived early. Her clock said 3 o'clock: it must have stopped.

"Footsteps sounded out heavily as they moved up the garden path towards the front door. Miss Pim made a mental note to speak to the newsagent—she didn't want the paperboy waking her, and her neighbours, with such excessively loud footsteps.

"Instead of stopping at the front door, as the paperboy always did, the footsteps continued to the side of the house. They were so heavy that when they came under her bedroom window, Miss Pim's bed shook. Now, half awake, and half asleep, her mind fluctuated between bewilderment and irritation at the paperboy.

"Suddenly, without reason or warning, when the footsteps reached the high wall at the back, they stopped. Miss Pim listened hard but they did not return. She looked again at her clock which said 3.20 a.m. The church had been ringing out the 3 a.m. hymn.

"The next morning Miss Pim looked around. The paper was, as usual, at the front door. She found no traces of any footprints or any attempted burglary, though she hardly expected such an incautious and noisy burglar. One of her neighbours had woken at the same time, hearing the same hymn and the slamming of the gate. She had not heard the footsteps.

"Miss Pim has never found any explanation for that night. Whether or not it has any connection with the house backing hers has never been proved, but this does have its own interesting story. It was owned by the Daniel family. During the Monmouth rebellion, the occupant, John Daniel [coincidentally the same name as that of the dead boy in the story set in the parish church] joined Monmouth and fled back to Beaminster when the peasant army was defeated at Sedgemoor in July 1685.

"Shortly afterwards the archangel Michael appeared to him in a dream, saying 'Go west'. He awoke to hear the noise of soldiers in the streets—soldiers hunting for rebels—who had tracked him down. As they had arrived at the front door he left by the back entrance, scaled the high wall and climbed down into what is now Miss Pim's garden. Then he fled to the family farm, three miles west of Beaminster. The soldiers followed him and he dashed into a barn and hid in a pile of hay, quick-wittedly grabbing a hen and taking it with him. When the soldiers began to search, and noticed the disturbance of the hay, he released the hen which scuttled out. The soldiers assumed she had been roosting in the hay, and left it."

BEAMINSTER

The Lady in Blue

BEAMINSTER'S MAJOR collection of ghosts are associated with the home of Monmouth rebel John Daniel. He lived at Bridge House, an attractive Tudor building which is one of the oldest in the town and stands at the corner of Whitcombe Street. Until the 1960s it was accompanied by another fine house nextdoor, Berith, but this fell during the decade of demolitions.

Amanda Allsop went to Beaminster in 1975 in search of the shared ghosts of Bridge House and Berith:

"At the beginning of this century the house was bought by a Mr. and Mrs. James. It was during their residence that the Lady in Blue appeared. Typically of Beaminster ghosts, she has no identity. There are no historical or dramatic explanations of her existence. Nor did she cause alarm, but seems to have been accepted as a matter of course. The first to see her was Evelyn Leigh, a friend of Mrs. James. She was staying with the family and at breakfast after her first night there, she asked why Mrs. James had been walking about the house so late at night in high-heeled shoes. Mrs. James was baffled and denied having done any such thing. The shoes attached themselves to a body, and a tall slim woman in a long blue dress—and high heeled shoes—began to appear frequently. Mrs. James used to spend a lot of time just sitting in the large hall and became quite accustomed to the companionship of the Lady in Blue. The lady seems to have stopped appearing in recent years.

"Around the time she disappeared from Bridge House, the house next door, Berith, was sold to the milk factory. The house had been owned by Mr. William Russell. He knew that the milk factory was after the site to extend their premises, and his dying request was that they should be resisted.

"His family held out for as long as they could, but eventually financial pressures forced them to sell Berith to the milk factory which soon demolished it. Just before the house was pulled down, two historians went to take the last photographic records. They took about twenty shots from various angles.

"When the film was developed, there appeared on two of the photographs—views of the front of the house, taken from the lawn—the distinct shape of a tall, slim woman in a long dress, wearing high-heeled shoes. There had been no one else present when the shots were taken, and neither man taking the photos was aware of any real or spiritual woman.

"The figure in the photographs fits perfectly the description of the Lady in Blue who had frequented Bridge House. It would seem that she had decided to transfer her haunt from the one house to the other. Now she is homeless."

Coincidentally, at the time Amanda Allsop was looking around Beaminster for ghosts I had a detailed letter from Mrs. Vera Newbery of Ludwell, near Shaftesbury, that gave her experiences of Bridge House and the story of a blood-stained ceiling:

"It was in the late 1930s when I arrived at Beaminster, to nurse an elderly and very sick lady at Bridge House. On my arrival I was given the Guest Room which was spacious and overlooked the stream and cottages on the other side of the road. Another window faced up the hill towards the Square.

"Early the first morning, something seemed to rouse me. It wasn't quite dawn, yet I couldn't sleep again and as the time trickled by I became more and more restless. Thinking it was the strange room and surroundings I gave it no more thought that day. However, this uncanny experience continued for many weeks until I moved into another room next to my patient.

"The daughter of the house, a very charging person, was arthritic and intended going to Bath for treatment. In the meantime she arranged for someone to take over the duties of housekeeper. The day came when the temporary housekeeper arrived. She was elderly and came from Walthamstow. After a brief look round the house she was given the Guest Room.

"During breakfast the following morning she was anxious to know if my patient and I had a good night, as she heard a distinct knock on the door of her bedroom and on answering it, found no one there! She said it was early morning and she hadn't been able to get back to sleep since. I felt sorry for her as I too had had the same experience; then I couldn't help thinking there's something odd, queer, about the Guest Room.

"On seeing the gardener, I spoke to him about it—thinking I might learn something, but all he said was, 'Ah, you be in love, that's what tis'. Bless me, I replied, then the housekeeper must be in love too!

"Well, about that time there were rumours of a second world war, and my patient's nephew arrived from Newfoundland to join the R.A.F. It was then the housekeeper decided to move into a back bedroom, for the nephew to have the Guest Room.

"That night things seemed to move with vengeance! I woke up to the sound of thuds, bangs, crashing and groans. It just terrified me—so much, I couldn't move.

"After we had breakfast, a very tired young man came downstairs full of apology for the commotion in the night. He said, he couldn't explain why or how he managed to fall out of bed without any bedclothes, and on doing so he knocked over the bedside table and smashed its lamp. The rest of the night he said was pretty miserable. Later that day he went to London to volunteer for the Royal Air Force.

"Both the housekeeper and myself felt convinced that the Guest Room was haunted and one day when we were discussing our experiences, the person who cleaned the polished silver arrived. It was then we learnt about the Ghost! She said her mother, before she was married, was in domestic service at Bridge House. All the staff knew that a murder had been committed in the bedroom over the dining room [the Guest Room]. The blood had seeped down through to the ceiling by the side of the beam and no one could ever remove the stain! Of course, we all went into the dining room to see if we could find the stain and there it was, a dirty cream looking patch.

"For all that, it was a lovely old house, and full of character. In the attic I was shown a trapdoor in the floor; you lifted it open with an iron ring and underneath was a circular stone stairway leading down between the walls which divided the kitchen from the dining room. There were several niches built in the stairway wall, suitable for placing things on. Someone said it was used as a hide-out presumably by Monmouth's men. Towards the end of the war, St. Dunstans used Melplash Court as a rehabilitation centre and Bridge House was taken over by one of their people after many interior alterations. I doubt if any of the old character remains or if the Ghost of the murdered lady still haunts those who sleep in the Guest Room."

BEAMINSTER

Scent of heroism

MOMENTS OF heroism during the inferno that devastated central Beaminster in 1684 may have left their impression on the town's folk memory. That would seem the likely source of two stories Amanda Allsop collected in 1975 from the old Market House Inn:

"The tuck shop standing on the side of Beaminster Market Square used to be the ostlery which served travellers to the market and overnight visitors who had come some distance with their produce. The building extends back a considerable distance: and the end room upstairs, now a sitting room long and low and beamed, has clearly been converted from a hayloft, above the stables themselves.

"In this room on winter Sunday afternoons, at about 4 p.m. there is the distinct smell of candle wax—of a candle which has just been snuffed out. The most down-to-earth unbelieving and unknowing people—residents and visitors—have experienced it.

"Two stories arise. The first is that at the beginning of the century, the lady of the house (after its conversion)—a not especially kind person—did make one heroic act. The house caught fire: she took a candle and went round the house warning her servants. She herself did not escape and was suffocated by the smoke, the candle extinguishing itself when she passed out.

"The second story is more romantic and would date from a much earlier period.

"In 1780 a new building was erected in the Market Place on the site of Beaminster's old Market House. This was a low unceilinged structure with five Ham-stone arches, in which the town's butchers set their stalls. In about 1818 the building changed its shape with the making of a long room above the arches, to be called the Town Hall, and the addition of a house and shop at the western end. By about 1850 the lessee of the shop obtained a licence for the sale of beer and cider, and this end of the building became the Market House Inn. It put up the same long-distance overnight visitors who stabled their horses at the ostlery.

"The building had long associations in the minds of Beaminster's older residents as the civic hub of the town, where they went to talk, to buy and sell.

"The Market House and its inn were demolished in 1886. Folk memories of a fire cannot refer to the eighteenth century building as there are no records of its having been burnt, only of demolition. But older tales from the days of its predecessor, the old Market House, may have become transferred and fused with the replacement building. Certainly, the entire centre of Beaminster was devastated by fire towards the end of the seventeeth century and a house overlooking the Market Place carries a yellow stone tablet in its wall: 'This town burnt in 1684. House rebuilt in 1687. W.L.'

"According to the story, a maid at the Market House Inn was betrothed to a young ostler, working in the facing building. One Sunday afternoon in November about 4 o'clock, fire broke out at the inn. The day was grey and overcast. The maid, aware of the rapidity with which fires spread among such intensively clustered buildings, took a candle and crossed to the ostlery to warn her fiance. By the time she reached the hayloft, she was too late—the building had caught and she expired in the fire. The candle snuffed out, leaving the perpetual memory of her tragic death in the form of the smell. There is also the possibility that she caused the fire in the ostlery herself—taking an uncovered flame into a wooden room full of hay is not the wisest thing to do."

BEAMINSTER

John Daniel's return

THIS STRANGE story, concerning a spectre which appeared in broad daylight and was seen by five children, is taken from a copy of the Gentleman's Magazine in 1774 where the narrative is prefaced as follows: "The intense pathos of the unfortunate and evidently murdered lad, reappearing amidst the scene of his childish occupations, and where he had been wont to play with those boys who could only look upon him as a passing shadow, is most suggestive."

The school at Beaminster, says the account, was held in a gallery of the parish church of St. Mary [Ordnance Survey map reference ST 478 013] and there was a direct entrance to this schoolroom from the churchyard. On Saturday, 27 June,

1728 the master dismissed the lads and twelve of them loitered in the churchyard to play ball. It was just about noon and one of the boys still had the key to the schoolroom.

Four of the youngsters entered the school to search for old pens and were startled to hear a noise which they described as that produced by striking a brass pan. They thought one of their number had hidden in the church and was trying to frighten them, but although the building was searched, no one was found.

The boys returned to their play but heard a second noise on the stairs leading up to the gallery and then, after running round to the west door, the sound of preaching succeeded by another sound like a congregation singing psalms. Again the boys resumed their game and, after a short time, one of them went into the school for his book—when he saw, only about six feet away, a coffin lying on one of the benches. He ran back, told his friends, and they all thronged to the school-door whence five of the twelve saw the apparition of John Daniel, who had been dead for more than seven weeks, sitting at some distance from the coffin, further into the school.

All of them saw the coffin and what seems to have prevented the seven from seeing the apparition was that the door was so narrow that they could not all approach it together. The first who recognised the ghost was Daniel's half-brother and he cried out: "There sits our John, with such a coat on as I have." In the lifetime of the deceased boy, the half-brothers were usually clothed alike. There was a pen in John's hand, a book before him, and the coffin to one side. "I'll throw a stone at him," said the half-brother. The other boys tried to stop him, but the stone was thrown, upon which John immediately disappeared.

This incident caused immense excitement in the town of Beaminster and the boys, who were aged between nine and twelve, were all magisterially examined by Colonel Broadrepp and all agreed in their stories, even to the hinges of the coffin; whilst their description of the coffin tallied exactly with that in which John had been buried. One of the witnesses was quite twelve years old and had entered the school after John had left it—and had not seen the boy in his lifetime.

This boy gave an exact description of John and continued to notice one point about the apparition which the others had not observed. He said there was a white cloth or bag round one of the hands. The woman who laid out the corpse for burial, later deposed on oath that she had taken such a white cloth from the boy's hand, it having been put there because of lameness about four days before his death.

John Daniel's body had been found in an obscure place in a field, about a furlong from his mother's house, and had been buried without an inquest, the mother having said the boy suffered from fits. After the appearance of the ghost, the corpse was exhumed and a coroner's inquest held, the verdict apparently being to the effect that the body had been "strangled". This verdict rested largely on the depositions of two women who told the court that they discovered a "black list" round the neck of the corpse, two days after it was found. The joiner who put the body in the coffin said the shroud was not placed in the normal way, but was in two pieces, one laid under and the other over the body. A "chirurgeon" who gave evidence could not, or would not, positively affirm to the jury that there was any dislocation of the neck. So far as can be learnt, no steps were taken to bring anyone to justice on account of the suggested death by violence of the lad, who provided one of the earliest yet best authenticated stories of an apparition in the West Country.

BEAMINSTER

Eloped to Gretna Green

A TALE of an elopement in 1790 is all that is now remembered to explain the occurrence of a phantom coach at Beaminster. It is another of the town's tales found for me by Amanda Allsop in 1975:

"The general absurdity and casualness of Beaminster ghosts is epitomised in the phantom coach which runs from Farrs, on the corner of the old Dorchester road, up towards Dorchester. The sound of horses' hooves clatter along the paving, though no apparition is actually visible.

"There is a story behind this. In 1790, Ann Symes, then twenty years old, eloped to Gretna Green with Samuel Cox of the Manor House. The garden door through which she eloped is still there, and is known as the wedding door. They were married at Gretna Green and later in Beaminster parish church, and subsequently produced a large family. The great-great-great grandchildren of one of their sons, Peter Cox, still owns and occupies Farrs. The descendants of their eldest son owned and occupied the Manor House until the early 1920s, when it was sold.

"Apparently the two families involved were of opposing political views—Whigs and Tories—hence the parental opposition to the marriage. But the opposition does not seem to have been strong. That they were married again in Beaminster, and inherited their parents' homes presupposes that all was soon forgiven. The elopement itself was ill-organised—the noises of the coach-horses would have woken the neighbourhood. Ann Symes's parents made no attempt to follow and stop them, so their objections could not have been great. Considering the general passivity and lack of drama surrounding the elopement, it seems odd that it should have left such a strong impression and be regularly recalled by the ghostly hoof-prints. But such is the character of Beaminster ghosts that they stubbornly refuse to fit into normal patterns of spiritual behaviour."

BETTISCOMBE

The non-Screaming Skull

AS BEFITS a good story, the saga of the Bettiscombe skull has lost nothing in the telling. What was to become the most famous piece of Dorset folklore first entered print in 1872 with the following words by John Symonds Udal:

"At a farmhouse in Dorsetshire at the present time, is carefully preserved a human skull, which has been there for a period long antecedent to the present tenancy. The peculiar superstition attaching to it is that if it be brought out of the house the house itself would rock to its foundations, whilst the person by whom such an act of desecration was committed would certainly die within the year. It is strangely suggestive of the power of this superstition that through many changes of tenancy and furniture the skull still holds its accustomed place 'unmoved and unremoved!'"

Udal later gave the location of the building with the ghostly tenant as Bettiscombe House, six miles north-west of Bridport. The skull, he added, had been pronounced to be that of a negro and the legend ran that it belonged to a faithful black servant of an early possessor of the property—a Pinney—who, having resided abroad for some years, brought home this memento of his humble follower. A serious collector of items of Dorset folklore, Udal—by profession a High Court judge—was furious to read that other writers, "had lent a somewhat heightened and conjectural aspect to the tradition." His informant had been an old lady who in her younger days had often visited and stayed at the old manor house at Bettiscombe. She also resented the new accounts of the story which held that the skull had been heard "screaming" and had added other innovations.

"So much for this sensational and, I believe, thoroughly unearned attribute of the very quiet-looking emblem of mortality known as the Bettiscombe skull," Udal wrote. He continued to recall his original visit to Bettiscombe House [Ordnance Survey map reference ST 402 003]. Conducted up a staircase, he arrived at a small door on the top landing and there was shown the skull. But this was not the original shrine of the skull and Udal took it up in his hands, picked his way through darkness up the attic stairs and entered the roof. There on a niche beside the huge chimney-breast lay a brick—and on this the learned judge placed the skull.

One of the stories Udal heard was about a former tenant of the farm who once, in incredulity or anger, threw the skull into a duck-pond opposite the house. A few mornings afterwards he was seen raking out the pond until he had fished up the skull, when it was returned to its old resting place in the roof of the house. It was said that the farmer had had a bad time of it during the interval and had been much disturbed by all kinds of noises.

The tale of the skull was to follow Udal across the Atlantic. In his capacity of Chief Justice of the Leeward Islands, he was in February 1903 on duty in Nevis. By chance he passed through a sugar plantation and was told it was called "Pinney's"—the name of its owners of a century before. Later in the week he visited Fig Tree church and found a handsome marble armorial slab, bearing a long inscription in memory of John Pinney who was born on 3 May, 1686, the only son and heir of Azariah Pinney. The Pinneys were a Puritan family of west Dorset and their arms were on the stone in the church. In England a brass plate on the wall of Bettiscombe church gave the name of "Azariah Pynney of Nevis".

Udal had established a link between Bettiscombe and Nevis, and was able later to prove that Azariah Pinney had joined the Monmouth rebellion, faced Judge Jeffreys at the Bloody Assize and was sentenced to be executed at Bridport. He was, however, upon payment of a ransom of £65 respited from execution and delivered a slave to Jerome Nipho. Azariah Pinney was one of the most fortunate of those transported after the abortive uprising; he soon ceased to be a slave, became a flourishing businessman employing his own slaves, and his son was eventually Chief Justice of Nevis.

John Frederick Pinney disposed of the family estates in the island about 1800 and returned to end his days in England. Udal mused, "May not one's imagination easily lead one to believe that it was the skull of old 'Bettiscombe', the slave purchased by him in 1765, taken by his old master with him to the very place, indeed, from which his trusty servant had taken his name, as a memento of his humble follower."

Though Udal was not given to fanciful theories, modern science later proved him wrong. A Professor of Human and Comparative Anatomy, Royal College of Surgeons, wrote in 1963:

"The skull is complete except for the mandible and a break in the left zygomatic arch. The whole bone structure is rather lightly made and the muscle markings are not prominent. It is probably a female skull aged between 25 and 30 years. . . . I think all these quantitative data lead to just one conclusion; that this is a normal European skull, a bit small in its overall dimensions but certainly not negroid."

This does confirm Udal's original opinion when he cast doubt as to the skull being of a negroid character at all. It was probably dug from a barrow on some west Dorset hill and brought to the house as a relic or *memento mori*, a skull displayed as a symbol of mortality. And yet the anatomical investigation goes some way to corroborate another piece of folklore. The skull was said to belong to a young lady who had died after a long period of confinement at the house— and near to its traditional resting place is a priest's hole type hiding-place fifteen feet by twelve feet, immediately under the tiles.

Dr. Anne Ross, lecturer in Celtic Studies at Southampton University, has been involved in the excavations of an Iron Age temple inside the fortifications on Pilsdon Pen, Dorset's highest hill. She has suggested a Druidic origin for the skull: "It was an extremely prominent part of the Celtic religion. The severed head was particularly significant. It was believed that the Celtic gods appeared there—that it was the seat of the soul. Skulls were supposed to have magical powers when connected with fertility. They were placed in wells for this purpose."

BLANDFORD

Dressed in crinoline

MISS L. F. PALMER of Wallington, Surrey, recounted the story of the crinolined ghost of Blandford, as told by her father, John H. Palmer, J.P. [1860–1952].

Before Mr. Palmer was born, his parents moved to an old house in Blandford and on a certain Sunday morning about the middle of the last century his mother went to church and, on returning went upstairs to her room to take off her shawl and bonnet. She turned and saw the apparition of a little old lady clad in black silk crinoline, standing near her bedside. Though the tiny lady looked harmless, and even benevolent, Mrs. Palmer was so terrified that she flew downstairs in panic and gasped out her story to her husband—who just didn't believe it.

A short time afterwards an aunt made an unexpected visit and had to share a bed with one of the children on the first night. About midnight she felt the bedclothes slipping off her, and thought the young girl had turned in her sleep. She rearranged them and was just falling into deep slumber when they slipped again, and this time she saw the tiny old lady trying to pull the bedclothes off. The aunt tremblingly got out of bed to rouse the family, but predictably fainted! Several similar incidents occurred in the next few months and the Palmers, deciding they could stand the house no longer, moved.

About this time, an unemployed baker entered the workhouse and the authorities, who seemed humane and considerate in Blandford, bought the old house to establish him again in trade. He prospered and was soon able to build his second oven, and even to buy a horse and cart. Townsfolk marvelled at his rapid financial recovery, but it was not till later in life that he divulged his well kept secret.

Soon after he had entered the premises, the little old lady appeared. Far from succumbing to terror, the baker watched her carefully and noted her wistful and worried looks, divining that she was anxious to recover long hidden treasure, once belonging either to her or her forebears. The baker considered a search might prove worthwhile and he raised floorboards, and dug in the garden; somewhere finding the means that made possible the enlargement of his ovens and the extension of his trade.

There are similarities between this and the story of the Shaftesbury monk who wanders the town to protect the hidden treasures of the abbey. What became of the little old lady isn't known; presumably once her secret was discovered the long vigil was over. The same, perhaps, may happen if ever the Shaftesbury riches are uncovered; the ghost will be lain.

BOURNEMOUTH

The spirit of Irene

MISS IRENE WILKINS, a young cook, was duped into coming from London to Bournemouth by a telegram sent from Boscombe Post Office. There had been two other decoy telegrams. They were to lure Irene to her killer, on the evening of 22 December 1921; her body was found the following day on wasteland, where it had been dragged from a car. Her end had been frenzied, leaving her skull smashed and her brains embedded with gorse prickles.

"The Great Bournemouth Mystery" the press dubbed it, as there was no obvious motive and no suspect.

The police were not, however, without clues. They had the imprint of a tyre from the motor car that the killer used. They also had Irene's case which had been thrown into bushes at Branksome. The murder weapon was not recovered but it was a blunt instrument such as a poker and the evidence pointed to a killing that took place indoors with subsequent dumping of the body. Her clothes were in disarray but apparently only because the body had been dragged through a barbed wire fence. There had been no personal or intimate assault—nothing 'sexual', as it would be phrased these days—and she was still wearing her bloomers.

There was also the killer's handwriting. Copies of the telegrams were printed in newspapers and shown on cinema screens. There was an overwhelming response with a total of 22,000 specimens of suspect handwriting being sent to Bournemouth police from all over the world.

Matters made no progress for several months. Meanwhile, from 31 January to 30 June 1922, local spiritualists held a succession of seances under the trance-mediumship of Mrs. Charlotte Starkey. After only a few minutes, at the first seance, she "began to show signs of a controlling influence, and she made for the case of clothes [Irene's, loaned by Superintendent Garrett] and took therefrom the stockings and from these she gave us the description of a man. Long sallow face, high cheek bones, dark brown hair, eyes hazel, medium height and build, big ears, weight 10 to 11 stone; he did not seem to be over 11 stone, and the sensitive gave details even to the size of the boots he wore. Not only did Irene gives us this description of the man, but other intelligences who controlled the medium gave corrobative evidence."

This account, entitled *The Spirit of Irene Speaks*, was compiled by William Tylar of Christchurch Road, Boscombe, and sold many thousands of copies in 1923.

"She said the hair was thrown up at the side, that he sometimes wore a lightish-coloured coat and a cap ... and that he also had a dark one with buttons and a driving coat—that he was a 'cute man but would not be cute enough'. The medium wanted to know who 'May' was as this name cropped up several times in the sittings ...

"On handling the coat, however, a change came over the scene, the medium being controlled, thrown upon the floor, and an impersonation of the death of the victim given. The body was absolutely rigid as though rigor mortis had set in. In going under control she gradually sank down upon the floor, shot her legs forward, and in some way this crumpling up and shortening of the medium's body resulted in the medium's clothes being drawn upwards till they were level to the knees. This was marked and significant, as the clothes of Irene were drawn right up to the waist when the body was discovered, the result of dragging the woman through the fence by pulling the ankles. The medium's body lay in the exact attitude in which the police found Irene. The legs were stretched apart, the feet turned toes outwards, the hand was clenched, and the clothes were somewhat pulled up towards the trunk. In a little time signs of returning consciousness were apparent; and the spirit professing to be Irene, who had taken control of the medium, spoke to us through her organism. The messages given were short messages in themselves, but collated and pieced together formed themselves into a clear and homogeneous whole."

One message was to the point. "You have him in your power, why don't you act?" Irene was said to have asked through Charlotte Starkey on 5 May 1922.

On 6 May, Thomas Henry Allaway, a Bournemouth chauffeur who had been held in Reading since 29 April—caught by his illiteracy as he tried to pass a dud cheque which he had signed "Arther"—was charged with the murder of Irene Wilkins. The writing on the cheque matched the Boscombe telegrams; these, too, had mis-spellings. Allaway, who denied the offence, lived with his wife, May, in Owls Road, in sight of the Burlington Hotel which was claimed to have been mentioned by the medium at one of the sittings:

"I've been running about a lot, I'm always along that road looking as if from the balcony of the Burlington." Mrs. Starkey was driven there, along Chessel Avenue. "Take me away," the medium protested. "Take me out of this. Take me out or I shall jump."

Thomas Allaway would be tried at Winchester and go to the hangman, though the spiritualists called for the abolition of the death penalty as absolutely contrary to the spirit of true Christianity.

"Someone else wanted her," Irene was said to have told the spiritualists, about herself, in a message implying that Allaway was a procurer. She described "a man who has travelled much and receives something from under the Crown". He owned a dog. William Tylar was circumspect about going further: "On this matter I can say no more."

Much to the embarrassment of the police they found there had been no need for any "Great Bournemouth Mystery". For Sergeant Fisher told Mr. Justice Avory that he had his attention drawn to the number of Allaway's car, LK 7405, at the beginning of January:

"I took a report from Mr. Humphries about the number of the car, on January 6th. I passed it on to Bournemouth Police Station."

It had been filed away. Something similar would happen with a crucial piece of evidence which could have caught the Yorkshire Ripper.

As for the spiritualist involvement, this was 1922—when gullible Sir Arthur Conan Doyle was lecturing on spirit photography in New York City and Harry Houdini and Joseph F. Rinn were exposing psychic fakers by offering wagers and duplicating seance tricks on the stage.

Yours Charlotte Starkey Sensitive

STUDY BY
REFLEX STUDIOS,
PARKSTONE.

BOURNEMOUTH [suburb of KINSON]/
HAMPRESTON [hamlet of LONGHAM]

Lady of the river

THE GHOST of a lady dressed in a long white dress and wearing an old-fashioned bonnet has been seen at various points near the River Stour at Longham and Kinson. Mrs. Ann Jorgensen of Nutley Way, Kinson, wrote to the Evening Echo at Bournemouth saying the figure had been seen "as recently as 5 November, 1971, when the young son of a Longham publican was heard screaming in the garden, terrified because he had seen a lady in a long white dress in the garden."

Hearing this, a Longham man was prompted to saying that "his neighbour had also seen a lady in a long white dress and wearing a bonnet, in his back garden while he was burning rubbish one evening." This man was so frightened by the experience "that he has not ventured into the back garden in the dark ever since." Traditionally, the woman is said to haunt the banks of the Stour at Longham.

But an identical figure used to be seen in one of the two cottages that formerly stood beside Wimborne Road a short distance west of the Bear Cross Hotel [Ordnance Survey map reference SZ 057 967]. Mrs. Gene Young of Haskells Road, Poole, recalled that as a small child she lived with her grandparents, Mr. and Mrs. Harry Penny, in this cottage. One day, as she was coming downstairs, Mrs. Young saw the old lady—"exactly as described" in the Longham sightings—on the staircase: "When I told my grandmother she told me it was an old lady named Mrs. Gridger who had lived in the house many years before. I only saw her once, but I can see her now in my mind as if it were yesterday."

The intriguing aspect of this case is that it suggests the ghost of Mrs. Gridger was made homeless when its cottage was demolished and has since materialised a mile away in the back gardens at Longham. These are the only old cottages left locally where it can still feel at home.

BOURNEMOUTH [suburb of KINSON]

Longham's chilling spectre

EARLY ONE frosty morning in February 1972, the Bournemouth Times reported later in the year, on 20 October, 30-year-old Robin Legg set off from his home at Berrans Avenue, Kinson, to cross the meadows towards Longham on his bicycle. He was riding along Millhams Lane [as it is always known; the council prefers 'Road'] below Kinson parish church, and was approaching the A348 on the south side of the River Stour [Ordnance Survey map reference SZ 064 972]: "It was about 5.30 a.m. and I'd just got to the end of the road. Suddenly—there in the gleam of my cycle lamp—was a greyish figure. I could see no face but distinctly made out some sort of cape which was flapping about. It was moving across the road towards some grassland at about normal walking speed.

"I jammed on my brakes hard. The road was icy—the bike slipped from under me—and I finished up on my backside on the ground. By the time I had looked again the figure had gone."

When Robin returned from work that day he was still certain about the incident and told Linda, his wife: "You're not going to believe me but I've seen a ghost!"

BRADFORD ABBAS

The bloodstains of the murdered gipsy

THE ROCK on the dark, dank sides of Bradford Hollow glistens in October with the bloodstains of a murdered gipsy. He is said to have been robbed and killed at night on his return, towards Yeovil, from the Pack Monday Fair in Sherborne. Bradford Hollow is a narrow, deep-cut ancient highway that has literally been sliced through the soft yellow sandstone above Yeovil to a depth of some fifteen feet. It is overhung by trees and ivy and lies on the south side of Babylon Hill [Ordnance Survey map reference ST 577 155] just below the golf course.

Professor James Buckman retired from Gloucestershire to Bradford Abbas in 1863 and recounted the story of the gipsy's bloodstains to one of his guests, Professor Lees, who was a micro-biologist. The following day they went to Bradford Hollow, a mile west from Buckman's house at Coombe, and scraped some samples off the stones.

It is a pity to spoil a good story, but Lees identified these as a cryptogamic species of vegetation which goes under the common name of gory dew. It has a red nucleus and a waxy appearance.

The story, as E. M. Garrett of Bradford Abbas reminded me in 1968, was never the same again but it refused to be completely laid to rest. There were, he said, still some villagers "who tell you in all sincerity that Bradford Hollow is haunted by the ghost of a murdered gipsy, and that bloodstains can still be seen at certain times."

BRYANSTON/DURWESTON

James Wyatt's Bryanston House: which the Portmans replaced with Norman Shaw's tasteless redbrick monstrosity (matching his New Scotland Yard) in the 1890s and thereby disturbed the ghost of .....

Aunt Charlotte

MRS. MARY E. BRADLEY of Durweston told me in the late 1960s about the Portman family coach. When, as a little girl, she went to live at the village she was told that at certain times of the year the lodge gates would open themselves and the phantom Portman coach could be seen making its way to Bryanston House. She considers the spectre is caused by the mist which rises from the meadows of the River Stour above Blandford between May and October, and across which flickers the light of the full moon.

There is a saying, "It is unlucky to uncover a ghost," and many claim that the fortunes of the Portman family changed when they pulled down their old house to build what became Bryanston School. Aunt Charlotte was the ghost they took for granted. A new kitchen maid came down to breakfast on her first morning and looked sick. When asked if she was ill, the servant replied: "No, but I woke up in the night and a lady in white came to my bedside and then walked out of the room." The maid was duly comforted and told: "Nobody takes notice of

Aunt Charlotte, she's often about but she won't hurt you." This lady was painted by Gainsborough and during the war our informant saw the picture at the top of the stairs in Knighton House, Durweston [Ordnance Survey map reference ST 857 082], when Lord Seymour Portman lived there. It has since been moved to the National Portrait Gallery.

Another explanation for the decline in the Portman family fortunes was that they sold their flocks of white and coloured peacocks. It was said that if the peacocks left Bryanston the Portmans would soon follow, as with the apes and the British at Gibraltar. The saying came true for the peacocks were sold by the third Viscount, and he died shortly afterwards, in 1923. The house and part of the estate went to the Crown Commissioners in lieu of death duties.

BURTON BRADSTOCK

Phantom dog of Cathole

A PHANTOM dog is said to cross Bredy Lane in the north-east corner of the parish of Burton Bradstock. Mrs. Muriel Aylott, who lived in Shipton Gorge in the 1920s, told me in 1969: "It's said that he came from a ditch, passed over from one side of the road and went into a hollow or a ditch on the other side. But I don't know anything more about it than that." The dog is said to cross the lane between Cathole Copse and Cathole Barn—"Cattle" the locals call it—which is three hundred yards north of Bredylane Cottage. It is a remote spot [Ordnance Survey map reference SY 505 906]. Some people say the dog is headless, but others that this part of the story has "walked" from the St Catherine's Cross coach story, located less than a mile to the north-west [listed under Shipton Gorge].

CATTISTOCK [hamlet of CHANTMARLE]

'Search for my bones,' the ghost of a murdered Scotsman used to shriek: an appropriate haunting for Chantmarle as it is now a Police college.

Bones of Wat Perkins

THE MAIN block of the fine yellow stone mansion of Chantmarle at Cattistock—built by John Strode in 1612 and now housing No 7 District Police Training College—had a ghost in its hall. Each year around 1825, at about the same date, a shrill piercing sound was heard in the hall, crying: "Search for the bones of Wat Perkins."

The words were repeated three times and brought fear to the house [Ordnance Survey map reference ST 558 022]. Accident, however, solved the mystery when labourers, removing a hedge near Kit Whistle—a cottage some distance from Chantmarle—uncovered a human skeleton, minus its head.

The workmen went to Kit Whistle where it appears that refreshments were then sold, and told the widow who occupied the house, of their discovery, to which she replied: "Don't say a word about it and I will give you the best cow I have." Her words did reach the authorities and upon interrogation she admitted, "If I must tell 'ee, the head is under the yeath stone," meaning the hearth-stone. The woman afterwards confessed that a Scotsman, who travelled with a pack of drapery twenty-two years previously, had come to her house and fallen asleep, resting his head on the arm of the settee.

She had chopped across his throat with a keen hook and had thus murdered him in order to steal his pack. In later years she had often said, when people were speaking of their clothing, that she "had burned better things than those." After this discovery, the legend goes, the old widow was tried and executed and the voice was heard no more.

CHARMOUTH

The monk and the white lady

R. W. J. PAVEY, in his *History of Charmouth*, tells of his mother's sighting of the white lady of Charmouth Lodge, an ancient house in The Street at Charmouth, prior to 1936. "Guests have complained," he writes, "that the door to the dressing room would open in the night." And there is a monk to keep her company.

A generation later, for the Dorset Evening Echo of 22 December 1971, Ellis Long interviewed one of the current residents of Charmouth Lodge—Miss Joan Whittington—who claimed direct descent from the famous Lord Mayor of London, the Dick of cat associations. "I saw the monk only a few months ago," she said, and added that his was a friendly visitation.

"Not so the White Lady, however," Ellis Long comments. "The story is that she was murdered and dropped down a well, the site of which is underneath the dining room floor. Her appearances are not so frequent and the last time was about twenty-two years ago." That manifestation was experienced by Miss Whittington's cousin, now the Rev. J. Robinson of Preston, Lancashire, who was playing the piano by candlelight in the dining room when the figure appeared and put her cold hand across his face.

"I can still hear his scream," Miss Whittington told Mr. Long. Her cousin suffered such a severe shock that he refused to enter the room again.

The lady is not confined to the dining room. Traditionally she was said to sweep down the stairs, wearing a full and flowing skirt, and through the flag-stone corridor into the garden. Although sightings had ceased with the frightening of the young man at the piano there was still the sound of footsteps along the passage ways after dark. The house has monastic associations and the other ghost, the monk, is said to appear in the garden. He is clad in a brown habit and is associated with the eve of a particular saint's day, though which is not specified.

The Priory's phantom stonemason

CHURCHGOERS AT Christchurch Priory in July 1972 had their services disturbed by inexplicable noises. A murmuring would follow through the choir stalls: "There's the phantom stonemason again."

The occurrences coincided with the time when mason Ian Sugg was restoring a Norman arch. But Mr. Sugg was always off work at the time of the tapping sounds, as one of the congregation explained to Evening Echo reporter Carl Whiteley: "I thought at first it was the stonemason working overtime. But he never works on Saturdays and Sundays. Then I thought it was something loose swinging in the wind and hitting the masonry. But it happens when there is no wind and when all the equipment is secured." Whiteley's story was carried by the Bournemouth paper on 24 July 1972.

Ian Sugg and the clerk of works, Norman Hoyle, faced particular difficulties with the arch. In Mr. Sugg's words: "We couldn't fathom how to key-down the stonework on the underside of the Norman arch to fit in with the window. We were stuck and just couldn't work it out."

This period of delay and indecision ended suddenly: "Then one morning both of us suddenly saw how it had to be done and the whole thing fell into place." Mr. Sugg would not claim divine guidance but did say: "One thing is sure. If we had been wrong, all the stones would have been too small and unusable. It would have taken a month to put right, plus the cost of extra stone."

The men also believed their workshop door, on the south side of the Priory, mysteriously opened in the night. Mr. Hoyle was certain the door had been securely shut the night before. In the morning it was open though "nothing had been taken and everything was in proper order".

Another time, whilst standing on the steps of the high altar with the head verger, Ron Smith, Mr. Hoyle could smell incense. "It was a distinct smell," said Mr. Smith. This surprised them both as incense is never used in the Priory. Tradition in Christchurch says the smell accompanies the ghost of Prior Draper who is said to walk the building at night. He was the last prior, at the time the monasteries were dissolved, and his tomb slab rests outside his own chapel in the Priory.

As for the vicar, Canon Leslie Yorke, he had not heard any mysterious tapping or experienced other phenomena but would not dismiss the stories: "There are many unaccountable noises in the Priory and I trust the integrity of those who tell me they have heard the tapping."

An ancient legend in the town links the Priory [Ordnance Survey map reference SZ 160 925] with St. Catherine's Hill, a steep-sided sandstone plateau to the north of Christchurch [map reference SZ 145 953] and separating the river flood plains of the Stour and the Avon. Building materials are said to have been supernaturally moved from the hilltop to the site of the present Priory by the harbour. In particular there was a beam, cut too short for the new building, that was sworn to have magically increased its length overnight. These pieces of folklore have some historical truth as they preserve the memory of an early Saxon church that stood two miles inland from the centre of mediaeval Christchurch.

Christchurch: the Priory overshadows riverside trees.

CHRISTCHURCH

Knocker's seasonal visitations to Somerford

MRS. ESTHER HORLOCK, who was aged fifty, and her daughter Anita (30) told the Christchurch Times in 1972 that for the previous five years, between the months of September and March, their home in Amethyst Road, Somerford, had been "plagued by a mystery hand rapping loudly on the windows and door". The paper carried the report on 13 October that year and Mrs. Horlock is quoted as saying that she refused to open the door of her council-owned house because there was always "nothing but fresh air on the other side".

She added that sometimes "I get so mad I swear at him or shout 'come on in, Knocker, there's a cup of tea waiting on the table.'"

The Horlocks said they had waited in the dark to ambush the culprit and would spread flour to catch his footprints. None was ever left, either there or in the soft earth of the garden which the Knocker would have to cross when he tapped on the windows instead.

Neither had the police any success in their efforts to catch the Knocker, Mrs. Horlock said: "Once a policeman spent all night at the house, but nothing happened. But on another occasion, when there was two of them, there was a knock. One of the policemen ran round to the back of the house but could find nothing."

The house was also occupied by Mrs. Horlock's husband and their children Jeffrey (15) and Lynda (13). Their married daughter, Mrs. Margaret Maidments (21) of South Bockhampton at Bransgore, also reported similar experiences from the time when she was living at Somerford: "I wouldn't stay in the house on my own. There was a knock once on the toilet window when I was in there—it gave me a terrible turn."

The presence was only active between September and March and also restricted its activity to the early part of the night, between 8 p.m. and 1 a.m. The family had appealed for help to their local clergyman, Rev. Rex Holyhead of St. Mary's at Somerford.

Mrs. Horlock was fearful of a recurrence: "I hate this house now. I can't settle down in the evenings any more. It's a really loud knock. Whatever it is, it's determined to be heard. I don't go out at night to hang up my washing. Nor will I go into the garden to get vegetables, as I used to. I won't even stay in the kitchen alone."

COLEHILL

A coffin in the road

SUNDAY'S BARN is the first building in open country that stands beside the B3078 Cranborne road out of Wimborne [Ordnance Survey map reference SU 011 014]. It is on the east side of the road about half a mile north of Walford Farm, on a slight rise that overlooks Catley Copse and a stream that flows down to the River Allen.

The sale of Sunday's Barn for a house conversion in 1986 revived memories that it gave a home to one of the "Dorsetshire Ghosts" recorded by Miss M. F. Billington in an article for the Dorset County Chronicle. A coffin is said to appear at the side of the road below the barn; I say the side of the road because I understand that a road widening scheme moved the carriageway a few yards to the west. The apparition is associated with the middle of the roadway as it used to be.

The origin of the story is a suicide who is said to have hanged himself in Sunday's Barn. I have been told he was buried, as was customary, with a stake through his heart in the middle of a crossroads nearly a mile to the north, below Higher Honeybrook Farm [map reference SU 010 026]. This is no-man's land, being the parish boundary between Colehill and Hinton Parva. The apparition of a coffin in the middle of the road preserves the folk memory of the poor man's fate.

CORFE CASTLE

The roof fell in

IN 1967 Mr. John Seager of the Halves Cottages, Corfe Castle, drove his van towards the bridge above Batterick's Mill on the south-east slope of Corfe Hill at 2.20 in the morning when he saw a figure in front of him [Ordnance Survey map reference SY 961 822]. At first he thought it was a woman in a nightgown out very late with her dog. As he drove closer, he braked hard. "There it was, a white figure, headless, and seemingly wearing a long nightgown, drifting across the road in front of me," he is reported as saying, in the Swanage Times of 12 July 1967. "It moved on and down the path at the foot of the castle hill, near the bakery. I trembled and came over cold, in fact I felt frozen. It was an experience I would never want again."

Some villagers believe the ghost might have come from the Manor House, at one time supposed to be haunted, and from which a secret underground passage is said to lead to the castle. Others, however, were doubtful as 22-year-old John told his story in the lounge bar of the Bankes Arms Hotel on a Thursday night. His leg was pulled about the ghost and John said he was sure something would happen if people didn't believe him. The room was cleared of customers and locked at 10.45 when, a few moments later, the whole ceiling collapsed, filling the room with half a ton of plaster and rubble. John, incidentally, worked in a Purbeck clay mine.

CORFE MULLEN

The Lavender Lady

Billy Heckford at Lavender Farm, Corfe Mullen, in 1959: he saw the Lavender Lady and the phantom coach of Corfe Lodge.

THE JACOBEAN manor house at Corfe Mullen, a tall building with high, round triple chimneys at each end, stands on the north side of the A35 [Ordnance Survey map reference SY 976 986] two miles west of Wimborne. The Phelips family of Montacute held the mediaeval estate and then intermarried with the Husseys who were lords of the manor until the English Civil War when one of them, "clad in velvet", fell for his king in a skirmish near Sherborne. They had strong fighting traditions. Nicholas Hussey was the last Englishman to hold the bastion of Rhodes, for the Knights Hospitallers [not the Knights Templars, as some Dorset histories wrongly claim], until it fell to brute force and Islam in 1522. When Thomas Hussey died in 1604 he left his son his "dromme and trompet . . . armour and implements of war".

The ghost of Corfe Lodge is, however, a kindly creature known as the Lavender Lady. Her story was told by Billy Heckford who was working at Lavender Farm in the 1950s. This farm, on the other side of the road, distilled the essence of lavender and roses for pot-pourri, sold in miniature "Dorset-owl"costrel-shaped pots made at Verwood, and tiny perfumed bricks for linen drawers. These were up-market products, sold at Liberty's and Heal's, though by the 1950s the famous farm had declined into a smallholding. Billy also claimed to have seen a spectral coach approaching Corfe Lodge and a figure dressed like John Bull. I have a photograph of Billy Heckford, at the age of 79 in August

1959, given by Mary Cliff, his niece, who was then bedridden and living near Ashburton, Devon. She provided a cutting of a letter she had published in the Poole and Dorset Herald, on 10 July 1969, which gave the full account of the ghostly lady who was called the Lavender Lady. Mary Cliff's mother was a maid at Corfe Lodge:

"My mother often told me about the ghostly lady at Corfe Lodge and I for one never doubted her word. She was a wonderful person, completely honest and sincere.

"She went to Corfe Lodge as a girl of sixteen. One night she was disturbed by footsteps and the opening of a door. Thinking it was her sister who slept in the same room, she called: 'Is that you, Annie?'

"Then she became aware that someone was standing at the foot of the bed. Looking up she saw this beautiful young woman, her hair in two long plaits, bending over the bed. The woman smiled and glided away.

"The next morning my mother wondered if she had dreamt all this, but several nights later the woman came again. When this happened a third time my mother became very frightened and refused to sleep in the room.

"She was then told that visitors to Corfe Lodge had seen the woman before, but no one had told her this for fear of scaring her.

"My uncle, too [Billy Heckford] saw the woman crossing the moor [the Stour meadows], and often spoke of seeing a coach and horses and a man dressed like John Bull in the lane leading to Corfe Lodge.

"I know these two people were too clear-minded and sincere to have imagined such things. The mystery remains, and I often wonder if later inhabitants of Corfe Lodge witnessed any strange happenings. I may be a sceptic over many things, but I know my mother's story was true. The Lavender Lady really did walk in the rooms of Corfe Lodge long ago."

DORCHESTER

The rector's ghost

CLERK HARDY and Ambrose Hunt, the sexton, had completed their task of decorating St. Peter's church, in High West Street, Dorchester, on Christmas Eve 1814. As they contemplated their day long labours in the icy building, they thought on how a glass of wine would do them good—temptation was there in the vestry, set out for the Holy Communion of Christmas Day, and their cups were filled.

Having sat down and taken the first sip, they became aware of a well-known figure sitting between them: their late rector, Rev. Nathaniel Templeman, who died the previous year. "He looked from one to the other with a very angry countenance, shaking his head at them just as he did in life when displeased, but with a more solemn aspect. Then rising and facing them he slowly floated up the north aisle and sank down gradually out of sight. The clerk swooned, the sexton tried to say the Lord's Prayer, and, when the apparition vanished he, after some trouble, unlocked the church door and got help for Hardy."

This version of the story is recorded in L. C. Boswell-Stone's *Memories and Traditions* [1895]. The rector, Rev. Henry Richman, heard of the incident which was soon known to everyone in the town. He considered their fright and shame to be punishment enough and did not dismiss the two churchwardens, neither of whom were later to recant their original impressions of that day.

DORCHESTER

The hotel creaking with atmosphere

IN 1955, Miss D. E. Warren was staying in The Antelope Hotel, in Dorchester, which reputedly housed the courtroom for Judge Jeffreys' Bloody Assize in the brutal aftermath to the Duke of Monmouth's 1685 rebellion. Miss Warren had been visiting the area to study prehistoric sites and it was at the Antelope itself on the site of major Roman buildings beside the town's forum that she experienced an extra-sensory incident that was still vivid twenty years later when recounted for Tom Perrott, the chairman of the Ghost Club:

"My room was at the back of the hotel. The window overlooked the room which was said to have been Jeffreys' courtroom. To the right I could see part of the alley and arch which led to the stabling in past days.

"On three nights running I was awakened by light streaming into my room, through an open door, from the passage outside. I thought that the lock must be loose and that it opened at the touch of anyone passing along the passage but it seemed firm enough. As it was a hotel rule for a light to be left on in all public passages I could do nothing but get out of bed again and close the door. To my amazement I found it open again on the third morning and mentioned it to the chamber-maid but she couldn't find anything wrong with it and as she looked at me a bit oddly I felt I shouldn't press the matter.

"The following night, in addition to the ever open door, I was awakened by the sound of footsteps going backwards and forwards in the room at the back of my bed-head. I heard an occasional chink of metal upon metal. I thought for heaven's sake what now? It was 2.30 a.m. and still the wretched pacing continued until in desperation I called out: 'For goodness sake shut up!'

"The noise ceased and the next morning I found that the adjoining room had been unoccupied during the night and had walls of a thickness which would have prevented me from hearing anyone. I sat down to consider what the whole thing could mean and just prayed it would stop. For my second week's stay the proprietor kindly let me have his daughter's room as she was on holiday. This was in one of the cottages in the coach-yard and for the rest of the time I slept like a log."

DORCHESTER

Shut that door

SINCE HIS childhood, Mr. Michael Legg accepted the existence of a ghost in the Old Malthouse, High East Street, Dorchester. The building, probably of the late eighteenth century, is of the local Broadmayne brick with some stone from the mediaeval Dorchester Castle and in the late 1960s became a store for antique furniture.   Mr. Legg described the phenomenon for me in 1968:

"It is not at all frightening and no one has ever seen anything, but footsteps are heard very distinctly and are often preceded by the sound of a door shutting.   I have heard this happening whilst the latch has been on the Malthouse door and at other times when the door is wide open.   From the door, the footsteps climb the stairs on to the first floor of the building and then fade away.   I have never heard them return down the stairs and out of the door."

These sounds have occurred throughout the time Mr. Legg has known the building but though the haunting conforms to its usual pattern there is no regularity as to when the footsteps may be expected.   Sometimes weeks go by without any strange sounds and then only days separate the occurrences.   Mr. Legg has known the footsteps to approach, pass and then continue behind him. On several occasions he has heard steps crossing the first floor, gone up to see if a customer was there, and found no one.   One explanation was that sound from the building next door, then the Noah's Ark alehouse, was conducted through wooden beams into the Malthouse.   The timbers of the Malthouse, however, run parallel to those of the inn, and the source of the sound is at the door and then along a line through the centre of the building.   The Old Malthouse lies beside an arm of the River Frome at the foot of High East Street, on the corner of High Street, Fordington.

DURWESTON

Sprinkled holy water

SOMETIME DURING the nineteenth century, children of Durweston told their mothers how they had seen a lady in black appear from a little door in the high wall that then surrounded the Rectory garden, opposite the church.   Little notice was taken of the ghost until these children who had seen the ghost started to sicken and die.   The epidemic was directly associated by superstitious minds with the sightings of the ghost.

The parish register apparently verifies the burial of about thirty children in quite a short period and the village was so concerned that an appeal was made to the Bishop of Salisbury who came and sprinkled holy water on the lawn and exorcised the ghost.   The lady in black was never seen again.

DURWESTON/IWERNE MINSTER

Two orphan girls

A WELL documented case of poltergeist activity first came to light on 11 January 1895 with this report in the Western Gazette:

"The little village of Durweston, three miles from Blandford, has been for some weeks past the scene of considerable excitement in consequence of the supposition that one of its cottages is haunted. The cottage in question is at Norton [Ordnance Survey map reference ST 852 089], a spot isolated from the rest of the village, some considerable distance from the highway and on the outskirts of a wood. The cottages are owned by Viscount Portman, his keeper (named Newman) occupies one, and the other until recently has been in the occupation of a widow (named Mrs. Best) and two little orphan girls, who were boarded out to Mrs. Best by the Hon. Misses Pitt of Stepleton. It is in the latter house that these occurrences took place, which have caused such a scare in the village. It is more than a month since Mrs. Best—who it may be here stated, is a most respectable woman, of a quiet inoffensive disposition and on good terms with her neighbours and the village generally—became puzzled by faint knocking and scratching in various parts of the house and could account for the same in no possible way . . ."

The Society for Psychical Research heard of the incidents and sent Mr. Westlake to investigate. He took statements from twenty witnesses and found the disturbances began on 13 December 1894. His most interesting interview was with Mr. Newman, the keeper, who was called next door on the 18th and told that Anne, the elder girl aged about thirteen, had seen a boot come from the garden and strike the back door. As he sat in Mrs. Best's cottage, Newman saw beads strike the window and he shouted back: "You're a coward—why don't you throw money."

The door then opened itself, to fifteen inches from the wall, and a quantity of little shells floated into the room. Newman continued:

"They came one at a time, at intervals varying from half-a-minute; they came very slowly and when they hit me I could hardly feel them. With the shells came two thimbles, they came so slowly that in the ordinary way they would have dropped long before reaching me. The two children were all the time in the room with me.

"Then right from below me a slate pencil came as if from the copper and a hasp, like the hasp of my glove, was dropped on to my lap from a point above the level of my head. I never saw any of the things start to move. The time was somewhere between 10 and 11 a.m. on a nice clear day.

"A boot then came from outside the door. It came in moving a foot above the ground and pitched down. The boot had been lying right in front of the door, where it had previously fallen. It fell just at my side. Mrs. Best threw it out. After this I went out and put my foot on it and said, 'I defy anything to move this boot'. Just as I stepped off, it rose up behind me and knocked my hat off. There was no one behind me. The boot and the hat fell down together."

A few days later the two girls and Mrs. Best, their foster mother, went to stay in Newman's cottage. Whilst they were there, the rector of Durweston, Rev. W. M. Anderson, and the schoolmaster, Mr. Sheppard, called on 10 January. Mrs. Best took the two children upstairs and put them in bed, lying there with them. Loud rappings were heard on the walls in different parts of the room and Sheppard went outside to ensure that no one was playing tricks. The rector remained, and a few days later wrote:

"I put my ear and head to the wall, but could not detect any vibrations. But when resting my head on the rail at the bottom of the bed, I could distinctly feel a vibration varying according to the loudness of the knocking. Occasionally there was noise in the wall, as if someone were scratching with their nails. When the rapping first began, I noticed that it frequently ceased when I came into the room, but after a short time it made no difference and the noise was loud and continuous."

The agency was invited to communicate by writing with chalk on a slate. This suggestion was answered in the affirmative by a number of raps and the slate was placed on the window sill. The poltergeist's condition of acceptance was that everyone except Mrs. Best and the two girls should leave the room, taking the light with them. The time was 2.30 a.m. and the witnesses waited below the stairs.

"Amid perfect silence we all heard the pencil scratching the slate," Mr. Anderson said. "The slightest movement by anyone in the bed would have been detected by me in a moment, and I am absolutely certain that the writing could not have been done by anyone in the room, without my knowing it. I told Mrs. Best that I was myself convinced that no one had moved in the bed, much less left it, but people would say such had been the case. She said she was prepared to take a solemn oath that none of them had moved or left the bed which was some four feet or more from the window."

Five times the group left the room. Each occasion brought scratches to the slate, once with a flourish of beautifully drawn curves such as a child could produce, and twice with actual words—MONY [sic] and GARDEN. No more was heard that night but the poltergeist was still very active and the two orphaned girls were taken to another home in the village, where raps and noises were heard, and were finally separated.

Anne Cleave, the elder child, was removed to the house of a spinster at Iwerne Minster—and there the disturbances again continued, noises being heard. A big stone was flung on the roof of the porch and snowdrops were strewn about the garden. Such trouble followed the unfortunate Anne that on 7 March Miss M. H. Mason, a Board Inspector responsible for foster children, came to Iwerne and took the girl to stay in her London flat for a week. No disturbances worth mentioning occurred during the week and Miss Mason had the child examined by a doctor who pronounced her of a markedly consumptive tendency and apparently hysterical. Anne's fate is not known but she had an elder sister who died about 1896 from tuberculosis of the lungs.

HAMPRESTON

Hampreston church: lit-up by corpse-candles.

Corpse candles

THE PARISH church at Hampreston, between Wimborne and Parley, is on a slight gravel rise but it stands only a few feet above the Stour meadows [Ordnance Survey map reference SZ 055 988]. Miss M. F. Billington, in an article on the ghosts of Dorsetshire for the Dorset County Chronicle in 1883, says that the church was regarded with supernatural dread because on certain nights of the year it was illuminated from the inside and the windows were lit with a "brilliant white light".

This, she thought, was the phenomenon of "corpse candles". Methane, from decaying bodies, would be particularly likely on damp soils. In the northern mining areas it is known as "firedamp" and treated with caution in any underground working or confined space. There was a reminder of its lethal potential in the early 1980s when a natural build-up from methane ripped apart a Lancashire pumping station and killed its party of open day visitors.

HAMPRESTON [suburb of FERNDOWN]

Poltergeist activity

THE MAIN story on the front page of the Poole and Dorset Herald on 17 July 1969 was headed: "Haunting shadows over their home." It told how Mr. and Mrs. Douglas Howarth live in a modern bungalow, built in 1963, which lies behind trees beside the line of the old Smugglers Walk at Ferndown to the north of Bournemouth. This track passes through a tunnel of trees close to Golf Links Road.

The Howarths told the reporter that they lived alone except for their dachshund, Skipper.

"Odd things are happening here," Mr. Howarth said.

The couple described how they had frequently heard slow, measured footsteps walking across the beams in the loft. Then there was the sound of a bedroom window being opened and closed. That was at two o'clock in the morning and Mrs. Howarth heard the window catch. Previously, during a meal, there was the sound of a package dropping through the letterbox. Skipper ran barking into the hall and Mrs. Howarth followed to collect the "post"—there was nothing on the mat.

Twice when Mr. Howarth had attempted to open the garage doors to put his car away at night one door—"despite being held open with a bolt firmly slotted into the ground"—had closed on him.

"That door cannot be moved unless one lifts the bolt, because I have tried to do it," he told the Herald reporter.

The bungalow, called Lohengrin, is near a copse which adjoins Smugglers Walk. There, too, Mr. Howarth had heard noises which he found difficult to describe: "When I hear this it is as if I were in a cloud for a few seconds—a kind of cold shroud."

The report ended by saying that Mrs. Howarth was the chairman of the Ferndown branch of Action for the Crippled Child. It is a strange case of poltergeist activity and one which is the more unusual because there was no young boy or girl living in the bungalow at the time.

In September 1972, when I asked Mrs. Iris Howarth if strange things were still happening, she said: "It still remains vaguely the same. A fortnight ago there was a similar incident. I was teaching a pupil at the time and we both heard what we thought was the back door opening and someone walking through the kitchen into the dining room. 'Is that your husband back?' the pupil asked, so I went to have a look although he wasn't due at that time. There was no-one there.

"We hear things like this but we never see anything. I wouldn't believe in this sort of thing but you can't get away from what you actually hear. It doesn't scare me, which I can't understand as I would normally be the first to be nervous."

HILTON

Watching the workers

AN EERIE stranger took a peculiar interest in building work being carried out near the Dorset downland village of Hilton, seven miles west of Blandford, in March 1973. Workmen constructing a reservoir for Dorset Water Board, to hold half a million gallons, came down from the windswept hill with stories of a ghostly cavalier which they had spotted several times on the site.

Reporter Ian Hunter, who was then living in Smithy Cottage at Hilton, wrote: "They told me the foreman who lives in a caravan on the hill had been touched by the ghoul late one night. On another occasion the cavalier clad in full royal regalia was seen standing on top of the reservoir watching the foreman."

The men were insistent and convincing, to the extent that Hunter was prepared to believe they had seen something, but when he spoke to the foreman he dismissed the weird happenings: "It's just a rumour that got out of hand. There's nothing in it."

Despite the denial, the foreman himself seemed to be "in a rather nervous state" and villagers recalled the legend that Oliver Cromwell's Roundheads had sacked nearby Royalist houses during the Civil War.

HOLNEST

Bedsteads flying downstairs

IN THE 1920s Mrs. Mowlem was living in the house which is now Higher Holnest Farm, to the west of the A352 five miles south of Sherborne [Ordnance Survey map reference ST 647 087]. She had an occult reputation that spread across the Blackmore Vale and the house was never without visitors. Edwin Short, who was 89-years-old when I interviewed him in 1972, recalled: "They came from miles, driving out in horses, carts, and carriages to visit this place. Things were happening there over a long period until she left and went to live in East Stour."

He had no doubts of how the house came to be synonymous with mystery and magic: "She was possessed of an evil spirit, I can't think anything else. Everyone said the place was haunted and that Mrs. Mowlem spoke to the ghost each night."

Mr. Short's father, George, had been carrying out building work on the Holnest estate since the days when it was owned by Dorset's notable nineteenth century eccentric, John Samuel Wanley Sawbridge Erle Drax. Once, said Edwin Short, his father called at Higher Holnest: "Father saw a door flung open and a bedstead come down the stairs piece by piece. He would vouch for that. The piano was also playing, on its own accord, with the hymn tune *Abide with Me*. He asked if that was all it could play and requested a dance tune. The piano obliged with this and the keys went up and down on their own."

George Short went on to receive a less convincing demonstration of psychic abilities in the kitchen. He was there to dig up the floor.

Mrs. Mowlem said she had spoken with the ghost and asked it: "In the Lord's name, what troubles you with this place?"

"If you care to know, follow me," the ghost is said to have replied. He proceeded to indicate the position of buried money under the kitchen floor. Mrs. Mowlem asked Mr. Short to do the digging: "Father dug it to two feet and failed to find anything. No matter, Mrs. Mowlem told him, the ghost must have moved it!"

The extent of the phenomena caused a welter of stories to be relayed through the Blackmore Vale and some are still recalled today. One is that the Mowlems employed a girl. She was once asked to go into the next room and bring a cheque from the sideboard, but as she moved to reach it, the cheque was snatched from her by an invisible hand. As with the other memories, this tends to categorise Higher Holnest as an incidence of poltergeist activity.

HORTON/HINTON MARTELL

Walking nun

MRS. DAPHNE LAWES of Coverack, Cornwall, told me in the 1960s that the ghost of a nun is reputed to walk along the lane between Horton and Hinton Martell, four miles north of Wimborne [Ordnance Survey map reference SU 023 063].

As far as she knew, it was last seen by Mrs. de Bary, the wife of the vicar of Horton, many years ago. There was once a small abbey of Benedictines at Horton, all trace of which has now disappeared, but according to John Leland it "was sumtyme an hedde monasterie, a celle to Shirburne". Another ghost seen to cross the road was a young boy in full Stuart period dress—who then vanished. This seems to be one of those areas with a host of ghost stories and I have it from two sources that the old rectory at Hinton Martell used to be haunted.

HURN [hamlet of EAST PARLEY]

The smokehouse secret

MARGARET KRAFT recalled for me how she used to feel "a miasma of misery" surrounding the smokehouse of a farm at East Parley. The year was 1939 and she was living in rural isolation at a spot that would shortly become Hurn Aerodrome.   Local people would tell her nothing about the smokehouse, though Mrs. Kraft was asked if she had seen anything.

"No, not seen," she replied.   "Only it's the feeling I get in and about the place—it's as if all the misery in the world is shut up there."

She was eventually told its secret.   In the 1840s, the Hungry Forties when England as well as Ireland was starving, children would raid these smokehouses for the sides of bacon that were hanging inside.   The point of entry was the smoke-vent in the roof.   The skinniest of the band would be lowered through the fumes, which rose from wood chippings, and secure a side of bacon to his rope. Meanwhile the lad had to grasp the hook on which the bacon had been hanging until the boys on the roof could lower the rope again for him to escape.

On this occasion something went wrong.   In the morning the farmer opened the door to replenish the fire and felt clothing as he turned the third of the sides on its hook.   The boy was hanging from the neck, his coarse clothing having caught in the hook at the point where the stolen side had been suspended.   He had suffocated in the fumes.

"There were, of course, those who hinted the farmer had caught the thieves at work and had executed his own rough justice," Mrs. Kraft writes.   "But whichever version was the true one, the lad was said to walk the path that ran along the garden boundary beyond the wattle and daub wall.   I never saw him, but I had no doubt his poor spirit lingered around the place, and I collected the tools [from the smokehouse] and locked the door once and for all, relieved to have the miserable business explained."

The story was published in issue seventeen of the Dorset County Magazine in 1971.

KINGSTON RUSSELL

Russells en route to Woburn

WHEN A notable aristocratic family loses its associations with a stately home then legend takes over to perpetuate the memory in the form of a spectral coach that is said to make regular visits up the drive to their former home.   Kingston Russell, a fine symmetrical Georgian house on the downs between Dorchester and Bridport [Ordnance Survey map reference SY 573 895] had a previous existence as the House of Russell.   The family have held the earldom and dukedom of Bedford from 1550 and 1694 respectively; they trace their descent from Henry Russell, a Weymouth wine merchant, who sat in four Parliaments from 1425 to 1442.

When the Russell coach returns to Kingston Russell House it is said that the members of the family, the four passengers, are headless—as are the four horses, the coachman and the footman.   The coach-and-four waits only momentarily at the door and does not unload its passengers.   The Russells stay aboard and go back down the drive.   They are on their way out, en route to Woburn Abbey, an old gentleman told me in Long Bredy many years ago.   It was just a tale, he said, which was of the sort that people used to like to half believe.

LANGTON LONG BLANDFORD

Ghostly horses

A TROOP of ghostly horses has been seen careering madly through Down Wood, about two miles out of Blandford on the B3082 road to Wimborne [Ordnance Survey map reference ST 910 068]. In the 1890s a man was coming home late at night and took a short cut through the trees. He had not heard of the legend but soon became aware of the frantic galloping of horses. Reasoning that they were the squire's horses, broken loose and engaging in some equine midnight frolic, he turned about and climbed through a hedge to leave the wood. The next morning he related his experiences in Blandford and was told of the haunted wood, to which he returned immediately, but there was no trace of a horse, no trampled bracken, and not a single hoof mark.

The Down Wood was almost completely felled in 1971 but the house at its centre still carried its name and by 1986 most of the tree coverage had regenerated.

LITTON CHENEY/LONG BREDY

Squire Light

BAGLAKE HOUSE at the east end of Litton Cheney village was, it is said, built by William Light of Baglake Farm. Squire Light went hunting one day in 1748, returned in a gloomy mood, and left the house again. His groom had a premonition that something was wrong and followed his master to a pond across the fields—to find the squire had already drowned himself. As the groom returned to the house, he was accosted by the spirit of his dead master, and thrown from his horse. He soon fell violently ill, and never recovered, one of the consequences of this illness being that his skin peeled entirely off.

Shortly after Squire Light's suicide his house—which he had built in about 1740—was troubled by noisy disturbances and a number of the clergy were called to exorcise the spirit and succeeded in inducing the ghost to confine itself to a chimney in the house for a number of years, after which the place remained at peace. Then, however, the power of the charm expired and worse disturbances broke out again with raps being heard at the front door, steps in the passage and on the stairs, and doors opening and closing. The rustle of ladies dressed in silk was audible in the drawing room and from that room the sound was traced to a summer-house in the garden. The crockery would all be violently moved, and at certain rare intervals a male figure, dressed in old-fashioned costume, is said to have made itself visible and walked about the house. These extraordinary occurrences were said to have continued for many years.

The main details in my account are taken from an article in the Dorset County Chronicle of August 1883 by Miss M. F. Billington, who names the building as

"Bagley House", a difference caused probably by local pronunciation. Baglake House, at the edge of Litton Cheney [Ordnance Survey map reference SY 555 906], is just over the parish boundary inside Long Bredy, at which church there is a record of the burial of William Light on 17 January, 1748.

LYME REGIS

Judge Jeffreys himself

LYME REGIS and its immediate environs have many ghosts of Monmouth and Judge Jeffreys origin. Yet one of the most bizarre of all concerns a Lyme ghost far from the town.

The Great House at Lyme is now known as Chatham House and has slipped into prosaic use as a shop and office block. It is a house of ancient foundation and sinister reputation. During the time of the Monmouth rising it was the home of a man named Jones. An ardent supporter of James II, he incurred hatred and horror in the Monmouth-supporting Lyme of 1685 by zealousy assisting Judge Jeffreys in his work of retribution after the rebellion's collapse. The heads of two of the Lyme men condemned as traitors at the Dorchester Assize are said to have been impaled on the spiked iron gates of the Great House.

The time came when Jones was dying, presumably from natural causes, in the Great House. "As he lay dead," the story goes, "there was a mighty noise and a great light in the air, and the gable of his house fell in, and the devil came to carry him away."

Whether he was removed soul and body, or soul alone, there is no mention but one would suppose Satan's main interest was in the soul. It is the second part of the Jones story that takes a different setting.

"Shortly after the master of a ship sailing near Sicily saw a strange craft looming in the sea-haze," the tale continues. He hailed it in the best British naval tradition but as it hove to—exemplifying another best British tradition of understatement—"he was a little taken aback to find it manned with devils."

A few centuries later, that master would doubtlessly have coolly demanded a sight of the Satanic Navicert as he prepared meanwhile for a round of shot across the stranger's bows if matters became tense. But this was the later 1600s and, so it would seem, the Satanic skipper was entirely forthcoming as he said: "Out of Lyme, bound for Mount Etna with Jones!"

The Lyme area is of interest to students of ghost-lore as the port suffered much both in the Monmouth rising and during the preceding Civil War. Even this story, despite its wide difference of detail and locale, does seem to fall in line with other ghost stories from the Lyme district. If these are sifted and dissected, they show a detectable origin in the seventeenth century and often carry suggestions of deserts escaped in this life being settled in the hereafter. In any internecine conflict—and those two were in quick succession—there are those deemed to have suffered unjustly, and others who in spite of their material prosperity have to live out their days under a cloud of suspicion.

There is a second ghost in the Great House—that of Judge Jeffreys himself. Tradition says he walks as a ghost wearing robes, wig, black cap and brandishing a bloody bone whenever the house, which stands in Broad Street, is empty. Even in recent years, with the building divided into offices and shops, the house has lost neither its reputation nor its mystery.

Heavy footsteps at night have been experienced by the staff who call the spirit Annie, while the older people of Lyme are more likely to blame the judge. One incident occurred in 1962 after the International Stores had closed in the evening and the manager was alone in the shop. He heard footsteps moving across the upstairs floor: knowing that both the estate agent's next door and Boots' the Chemist were closed at the time, the manager investigated. He searched the building but found no intruder. This and other stories about their Lyme shop became so well known among International Stores' workers at other branches that the tale was even printed in the company's own magazine.

Jeffreys and his other judges visited Lyme on 11 September 1685—the next day twelve of Monmouth's men were executed on the beach west of the Cobb where their leader had landed three months previously. The party probably stayed not at the Great House but with the mayor. He dined them with half a cage of sturgeon and 15 gallons of wine. Lyme's mayor was later surcharged the £25 cost of this "treat to my Lord Chief Justice and the other judges."

LYME REGIS

Something very cold

MRS. W. BIRD of 36 Coombe Street, Lyme Regis, told a reporter for the Bridport News in 1967 she thought her house was haunted as she had seen a figure which disappeared, standing beside her bed. The story might have been an instance of poltergeist activity but is of most interest as it led to other people in Lyme informing the newspaper of ghostly incidents. "The name of the Angel Inn seems to crop up time and time again," said the paper.

A former resident, a lady, is supposed to walk about the house and one person prepared to believe the tale was Mr. Joe Wain who worked for his father-in-law, Mr. Ted Oaks, the landlord. The paper continues to say that Mr. Wain, who is described as a tough rugged, former lorry driver, admitted that he was "frightened to death" when, one day in 1966, he went into a bedroom to fetch a snuff-box for Mr. Oaks. "Something very cold suddenly came over me," he said, "it was a terrible experience and even the dog, Sheena, is frightened to go upstairs. She sleeps downstairs under the mat."

LYME REGIS

Afraid to work alone

BOTH THE Royal Lion Hotel and Lyme Regis Printing Company in Broad Street, Lyme Regis, were plagued by a poltergeist in the summer of 1973. So sure was the printing works manager, Michael Woodward, of supernatural activities that he told Clare Millero, a reporter, he would welcome a visit from an exorcist.

"I was working in the upstairs department the other night," Mr. Woodward said in July, "on my own and I heard somebody whispering about ten feet away. It seemed to go away towards the end of the room. Then doors started banging downstairs and the internal phone started ringing. There was nobody in the premises nor in the flat, and there was no technical fault with the phones."

Similar events had also happened to the foreman, Philip Curtis, and neither men would work alone at night again. A machine operator had heard banging and crashing from an upstairs room when he was the only person in the building. Another member of the staff heard doors banging and the ticking of a non-existent clock. Once Mr. Woodward walked upstairs and felt he was entering an ice-box. Downstairs it had been warm.

Mr. Curtis described his experiences: "There used to be two doors upstairs which were bolted. Sometimes the bolts were found to be undone and the doors open when I went upstairs. I have also heard footsteps going across the flat."

The New Inn, another Broad Street building, also figured in ghostly stories before its closure early in the 1960s. In 1973 it was the turn of the Royal Lion. Two young couples were working there, Alan and Susan Jones, and Markus and Geraldine de Roseus. Late one night, Alan went into the kitchen for some blackberry pie: "Hearing a door close and footsteps coming across the dining room, he went through to see who it was. No one was there."

Markus also had an experience in the dining room when he heard the kitchen door close and footsteps approaching him across the darkened room. Terrified, he ran outside: "I've been frightened in my life before, but never anything like this."

The four employees had all felt a cold and chilling sensation at the times of these occurrences. "It's like a damp mist going right through you, turning you to jelly," was how Susan put it. From their bedrooms on opposite sides of the courtyard, both couples had heard "the eerie moaning of a woman endlessly through the night". Organ music also occurred.

Items, particularly religious or charms for good luck, had been disappearing and Geraldine was amazed to witness a beer glass slide over and smash on to the carpeted floor of her bedroom. The hotel receptionist was equally surprised when cigarettes shot out across the room from a packet which had been resting on the wide arm of her chair. Once, Alan and Susan saw a white shape "like a drifting mist or steam." "We're all frightened to death," said Alan, "We just can't understand it."

The Royal Lion is a large three-storey building that includes sixteenth and seventeenth century beams and partitions in its lower floors. Next door is said to have stood Lyme's courthouse and the yard is reputed to have been the scene of the occasional hanging.

The 1973 reports appeared in the Bridport News on 13 July and 3 August.

LYME REGIS/UPLYME

Black Dog Lane

ACCORDING TO Gaelic legend "there is a gigantic black pig which one day will swallow the Earth," thus making an end of it and all upon it. This pig story is believed by some to be one of the origins of the "ghostly black dog" stories which are common over most of the British Isles and particularly English counties with a seaboard.   Another origin, especially in coastal districts, may be the legend of the war hound of Odin—"the Viking Hound of Odin, the might Dog of War"—who came to this country with the invading longships as the Roman hold upon Britain began to weaken, leaving the North Sea coastline, and the eastern end of the Channel exposed to attacks ranging from those merely intent on plunder of the sea borne smash-and-grab order, to more serious efforts at territorial conquest.   Some maintain that the "ghostly black dog" entered Britain by way of "the East Anglian bulge" (probably Suffolk, the scene of many of the major Viking landings) and from East Anglia came one of its most commonly used names, the "Galleytrot".

Similar stories may have come into England from time to time by way of fugitives from religious persecutions on the continent, for they also exist in France—the "hunt macabre"—and in Germany—"the wild hunt."   From Germany, too, may have come an admixture of werewolf tales as well.   Although stories of the apparition follow, in general terms, an overall pattern, yet within that pattern there are sundry local variations.   Sometimes the black dog is merely reclining by the roadside, a fairly large creature, and unidentifiable as to any current breed of dog.   Sometimes it is galloping or running along the road, never, apparently, taking any heed of anyone it may meet, either by moving, if recumbent, or deviating its courses.   Neither, apparently, does its sighting presage anything of moment, such as national or individual disaster.   Its appearances would seem without special purport.

South-west England has numerous "ghostly black dog" stories.   In Cornwall there is an association with the devil, and judging from the name "the Devil and his dandy dogs" more than one dog is involved.   Several stories run along those lines, most belonging to lonelier moorlands, which they sometimes are said to frequent.   Dartmoor has its "Ghostly Hound of Dartmoor," a fairly large creature with plenty of accounts of sightings current during last century.   Incidentally, Conan Doyle's famous Sherlock Holmes novel, "The Hound of the Baskervilles" is based on the exploitation for dubious ends of such a Dartmoor story.   In north Devon, too, there is the "Black Dog of Torrington," again an apparition following general "Galleytrot" lines, but apparently not seen of more recent years.

One of the best-known and best documented ghostly black dog stories of the South-west is shared between Devon and Dorset, for it belongs where these two counties meet with Dorset's Lyme Regis merging into Devon's Uplyme [Ordnance Survey map reference SY 331 930].   It makes it on to the map at Black Dog Lane—its venue—and is also honoured by the Black Dog Inn on the main road running down into Lyme (more or less in parallel with Black Dog Lane).   It is a lane which used to be studiously avoided even by quite hardy-minded locals after dark.   Even today there are those who declare it is haunted by that black dog "which is seen at dusk, always approaching, at first sight no more than any ordinary smallish black dog trotting along on its own.   But as it gets nearer it quickly gets bigger and bigger until it is enormous.   Then it has gone."

The most detailed story of the Black Dog of Black Dog Lane belongs to around the close of the last century and was told by one of the coastguards from Lyme. In Black Dog Lane one evening at dusk he noticed a little black dog approaching him, taking no more heed of it than he would have done of any other little dog running along by the side of the road. Then he noticed it was getting bigger and bigger, turning into a kind of gigantic black cloud. Gathering speed, it was above him and all around him, passing by him as if he were not there—and gone.

[This piece was written by Mary Collier and myself for *Ghosts of Dorset, Devon and Somerset*, 1974.]

LYTCHETT MATRAVERS

Voices of Whispering Corner

MARY COLLIER told me about her experiences at Lytchett Matravers for inclusion in *Ghosts of Dorset, Devon and Somerset* which we compiled with the help of Tom Perrott in 1974. This is the account in her words: "July and a bright high-noon. Climbing up the hot and dusty Church Path at Lytchett Matravers near Poole, thinking of the adders infesting it rather than the voices of its mysterious Whispering Corner, I coughed. I announced my presence, for, from the sound of voices ahead I must be intruding on somebody, most likely love's young dream making the most of its lunch-hour. But nobody was there.

"The whispering continued. All around rather than from one single place, part of the woods and the hillside itself. Voice or voices, male or female, it was impossible to distinguish. Continuous, its volume sometimes rising and falling a little, sometimes a little breathless: definitely the sound was of the human voice. Hardly the traditional hour of ghosts, yet I seemed to be hearing one, or more than one, loud and clear into the bargain. The most perplexing aspect was that, try as I might, I could distinguish no words. If words were, indeed, being formed, they were in a language unknown to me.

"The Church Path at Lytchett Matravers [Ordnance Survey map reference SY 936 962] is the footpath to its ancient, Norman-towered church. Turning off the road by way of a gateposted entrance, skirting a wood, it emerges on to a small plateau on the hillside. Then, the woods still flanking it on one side, farmlands on the other, these, themselves, skirted by still more woods, it takes a sharp right-angle turn, cleaving its time-honoured way down the steep hillside to the valley where the church stands, and where, too, the Manor House of Lytchett Matravers used to stand. Today only the site of that house remains.

"From long before the Domesday Book, in which it is mentioned, that site had held homesteads. The Manor House site was once the home of Sir John Maltravers who took part in the killing of Edward II. The king died with a red-hot poker thrust into his anus. Maltravers passed away peacefully in 1365 and is buried, reputedly in full armour, in the church which still carries his name. His brass lies on the floor of the north aisle at St. Mary's, Lytchett Matravers.

"Ghost stories galore—or perhaps better described as yarns about spooks— clung around the house itself, its grounds, and its surrounding terrain. During the some four years I lived at the Manor House, converted into flats in its final days, I had indulged in sundry privy ghost-hunts, for that ghosts existed I had little doubt. But what, or who, were the ghosts of the Manor?

"Certainly they were not the alarming apparitions that somebody else's mother, grandmother, great-uncle, or second cousin by marriage several times removed had thought they had seen, but which served, nevertheless, to scare away most of the villagers from the Manor and its immediate—even less immediate—environs after dark; for that matter from the Church Path, too. These particular ghosts were numerous, something that one felt rather than saw, 'presences,' that were friendly spirits. Many times, both in daylight and after dusk had fallen, I had passed Whispering Corner, often hearing the odd whisper, taking little heed of it. That whispering ghost, or ghosts, was part of the Church Path. That was how I had been brought up to regard ghosts, accepting their existence as something as normal and unremarkable as my packet of cereal.

"Of the many theories put forward about Whispering Corner—that is, the non-ghostly ones—none really seemed to fit. The more logical hovered between some subterranean watercourse or spring, its sounds amplified and refracted in hollows along its way, and some trick of acoustics in the basin of the hills. Both were plausible; the spring-fed reservoir serving the Manor was in the nearby woods, although lower down the Church Path than Whispering Corner. Within that bowl of the hills was one of the clearest and most remarkable echoes I have ever met, but only at its maximum effect at certain special points, not on the Church Path itself, but from the surrounding fields, one spot being in a field forming part of the Manor grounds. An elderly local resident with many a story of the Manor and its surroundings to tell, introduced me to these, demonstrating how, even a foot or two away from the precise spots, the echo lost its power. But from those precise spots one could send one's voice ringing round and around the hills, echoing and re-echoing until finally it went where all good echoes go.

"Although these theories as to the possible physical origin of the whispering cropped up often enough in conversation, particularly if someone had recently heard a 'voice,' we had no effective practical means of putting them to the test. Admittedly they were fairly long shots, just as long, maybe, as most of the others and less plausible notions, with probably the whole lot of them wide of the mark. All of us, I think, felt a sense of confrontation with something beyond the purely physical, but how far commonsense prevailed there, or was over-awed by the admittedly somewhat spooky ambience of the valley in general, I, for one, can't affirm. Perhaps we were, consequently, conditioned to accept the supernatural without applying to it the hardheaded reasoning of our backgrounds and professions.

"Be that as it may, the setting for the supra-normal was there, for that deserted bowl of the hills once held the mediaeval village of Lytchett Matravers. Its presence is still betrayed by grass-grown hummocks breaking the smooth contour of the slopes and there are other odd undulations in the still-wooded folds. That village of Lytchett Matravers, clustering around its church and Manor and drawing its being from the fertile and well-watered valley, was decimated by the Black Death, the scourge of mediaeval Europe for generation after generation. Mostly the plague struck in the confined and insanitary conditions of towns, from which refugees brought gruesome stories, and infection as well, to the villages where they fled.

"The plague was known in France as 'le fléau' [the flail] and in England it was simply 'The Death'. It entered this country through the Dorset ports of Melcombe and Weymouth at 'about the Feast of the Translation of St. Thomas,' the

July, that is, of 1348.

"One popular precaution against infection was sniffing up smells from the outlets of privies. This was a kind of crude forerunner of inoculation, intended to immunise by providing doses of the malady one is trying to avoid. Probably, though, it only helped to spread the plague.

"The South-west was one of Britain's worst-stricken areas with Lytchett Matravers, down in the shelter of its well-tilled valley, one of the worst-stricken villages. Panic seized the handful of survivors. That valley was holding the plague and they could only flee to the hills above Poole Harbour and hope that the sea winds would blow it from their bodies.

"One of the routes they would certainly have taken in their flight to the wind-girt hills, perhaps, even, the sole one, would have been the Church Path. Survivors probably sick themselves, toiling up its slope bearing other sick and maybe the dying with them, resting awhile on that kindly half-way house of the plateau now called Whispering Corner, comforting each other in voices hushed by fatigue and fear, awed by sorrow for their loved ones lying, unburied, in their deserted homesteads still so close to them, waiting for fox and owl to grant them their last rites. Even today their bark and screech as darkness falls are an eerie reminder of the village that was, in the valley of contamination.

"For some mysterious reason, still the subject of historians' surmise, no one ever returned to the deserted village. A new village grew up on the site of the Lytchett Matravers of today. Normally economic reasons dictated a return when the plague had abated, over-riding whatever emotional compunction might exist to restoring the thread of their old lives, for on the husbandry of their established farmlands hung whether folk ate or starved. Yet that valley remained a place of uncleanliness, a haunt of the unburied dead, of mournful shades mingling with the mists drifting in from the estuaries of Poole Harbour, clinging around the tree-tops on the lonely hillsides as the ultimate mercy of briar and bracken enshrouded the place they had once called home.

"Are theirs the voices of Whispering Corner? Does the anguish of the fleeing still cling to that spot where they bade their farewells? Ask the older residents and come out by that same door where in one went: 'There's always whispering there. Always has been as long as anyone can remember. No one knows who or what it is, and you may hear it at any time. Oh, yes! Whispering Corner's haunted right enough! No doubt about that, and for that matter so are the valley where the village used to be and the Manor House itself. Nobody'll go anywhere down there after dark and there're some who don't even fancy it by daylight!'

"Moving into Devon some years later with Whispering Corner far from my thoughts, a friend living near Branscombe remarked one day 'we've got a stream near here with a water-spirit. Spirits follow water, you know, it seems to attract them in some way, I don't know why. Yes, I suppose you'd call me psychic or somewhat so—I'm a dowser, anyway. I've always felt a 'something' about that stream, and there's a field, too, we call Pan's Field. One day a friend and I heard a voice whispering by the stream—quite a distinct whisper—and then we felt sure that the 'something' is a water-spirit.'

"Whispering Corner sprang to my mind: 'I think I've heard a water-spirit, too! Whispering, and whispering quite loudly.'

"'Could you distinguish any words? We couldn't.'

"'Not one,' I replied, 'but I'm thinking—wouldn't it have been some very long past language?   Wasn't Sylvanus the god of the springs?'

"Had Whispering Corner found its answer?   Sylvanus, the god the occupying Romans prayed to along with Mithras; the god who kept the streams running to water their lands.   'Sylvanus was good enough for my father and grandfather before him.   He's good enough for me!' declared the more cautious when confronted with Christianity.   'Somebody or something got him into a huff the other summer and you remember what happened then!'   Better to play safe than to dry up.   Was that answer far older than the Black Death, even than the Domesday Book, for that valley is also believed to have been the site of a Roman homestead, probably owned by one of the wealthy families with their culture still in Rome but their lands in Britain.

"Still part of Roman life when the legions left Britain, Sylvanus was but one of his names, for he had always been part of the rising springs, old as sweet waters themselves, his spirit their spirit, his speech the tongue of earth and sky, of light and darkness, of the things of the earth and its waters.

"Whisper on, Whispering Corner!   I, for one, have no answer."

LYTCHETT MATRAVERS [hamlet of HUNTICK]

Night of terror

NOT FAR from Huntick at Lytchett Matravers, north-west of Poole, is a plantation with a belt of fir trees along the road [Ordnance Survey map reference SY 958 950].   Opposite were dotted a few old farmhouses and in one of these, at the middle of the nineteenth century, lived some people by the name of Cresley.

One of the sons, a soldier, had gone to camp and was not expected to return on that evening so the family locked up and went to bed.   The son, however, was able to get away from camp and at two o'clock in the morning he was two hundred yards from home when he suddenly heard the sound of bells ringing and was startled to see a shadowy figure emerging from the wood.   Terribly alarmed, he started to run and the apparition followed him, constantly muttering as the bells clanged.   In his terror, the young man did not wait to be let in, but burst open the farmhouse door with the sheer weight of his body.   He then turned to see the ghost gazing through the doorway at him.

The sound of the bells had awakened the household and the soldier's mother, braver than the rest, looked out of the window and saw the ghost standing there. She watched until it vanished; it seemed not to go anywhere but simply to disappear.   Through the plantation, from where it emerged, runs an old road. The road from Lytchett Matravers towards Poole crosses Huntick Hill and there are several rumours that it is haunted.   The children used to tell each other, as maybe they still do, that a mourning coach came out from among a small wood of holly trees and went up and down the road.

About 1900 a man declared that one night as he was returning home very late he first heard a vehicle coming behind him and then saw pass a brilliantly lighted coach drawn by two horses.   It went on a little way, stopped, met and passed him again.   There was no cause for fear and the man asserted that it was the most beautiful sight he ever saw.

Another incident was seen by Billy Bartlett early in the nineteenth century when he beheld at dead of night a complete funeral cortège on the Huntick Hill road. Billy was greatly impressed by the ghostly mourners carrying lighted tapers.

I cannot decide on the validity of these stories as Huntick Hill is a key point on one of the most used smuggling routes away from Poole landing areas. Most of the Huntick traditions date from before 1850, a time when local superstitions were exploited to the full by the bands of smugglers to discourage country people from straying abroad at night. There is even, by coincidence, a story of the enterprising and notorious free-trader Isaac Gulliver moving kegs away from West Howe in a funeral coach at night.

MARNHULL/TODBER

Legendary battlefield

TWO BEARERS, their faces hidden beneath the pall that covered the coffin, were supposed to be seen at midnight crossing Sackmore Lane, Marnhull, on a certain date. The tradition asserts that no procession of mourning followed the coffin, whose bearers went towards a legendary battlefield near Todber, close to a limestone quarry, where in 1870 a large quantity of human bones were unearthed, which rather indicates that there had been a battle after all.

Another Marnhull story, also in *The Marn'll Book* [1952], holds that a cottage in Burton Street was once the home of Michael Harding, a shoemaker. The sound of rapid hammering was heard nightly until someone in the house asked: "What 'ave 'e lost tonight, Michael, yer hammer?" The ghost never returned.

Cottages were formerly where Ashley Farm stands now [Ordnance Survey map reference ST 787 195], and it was in front of the fireplace in one of these, that a man used to appear in breeches, gaiters, long tail coat and brass buttons. This is another instance of a ghost guarding a hidden treasure as, when the cottages were demolished, a hoard of coins was found under the hearth stone.

MARSHWOOD [hamlet of FILFORD]

The Quaker Oat Man

IN 1969 MRS. Muriel Aylott, who was living near Redhill Common at Bournemouth, recounted for me an experience which happened about 1918, when she was aged seven or eight, but which was so vivid that it has remained with her ever since. At that time her grandparents lived and farmed at Higher Filford Farm [Ordnance Survey map reference SY 439 975], in the west Dorset parish of Marshwood, between Bridport and Broadwindsor.

Mrs. Aylott, with her brother and sister spent many holidays at this seventeenth century house and one day decided they would explore a dark passage and open a door at the end—an adventure they had been forbidden to undertake.

Ensuring their grandmother, who used the passage to reach the cheese room where large mature and ripening cheeses were prepared for market, was not about, the children set off, taking care that the stairs did not creak. They were able to creep along the passage and ease open the door, to see the latticed windows which were always kept closed and a figure sitting looking in their direction with the thumb of his right hand resting in the fork of a stick that stood on the floor; the Quaker Oat Man. He was dressed exactly as the man on a packet of Quaker Oats, with an old greyish-looking coat with silver buttons, and epaulettes on the shoulders. He had on his head a tricorn hat which was turned up at the sides—the figure was bearded and looked very old, probably over eighty.

The children chorused, "Hello". To this the old man, his long, knotted stick and all, disappeared backwards through the wall.

The time was early evening and the children told the incident to the grandparents, who severely reprimanded them and promised them the biggest walloping of their lives if ever they ventured near the cheese room again. Even thirty years later, other relatives refused to discuss the incident and would only say: "Oh yes. We knew about it. We knew about your Quaker Oat Man."

MELBURY BUBB/EVERSHOT

Thomas Baker's horse and cart

IN MELBURY BUBB churchyard there is a broken tombstone inscribed to farmer Thomas Baker "elivs [alias] William who was baberovsly murdered on Bybdowne Hill November 10 1694". He had ridden across the seven hundred foot high Bubb Down Hill [Ordnance Survey map reference ST 589 060] with two bags of golden guineas slung across his saddle. The two murderers escaped for seven years and were then heard arguing in the Acorn Inn at Evershot about Baker's death.

The next day they were taken, manacled, along Long Ash Lane which is now the straight stretch of the A37 over the Dorset Downs to the Frome valley and Dorchester. There, in 1701, they were sentenced to be executed at "the tree by which they did commit wilful murder, there to be gibbeted in chains to suffer death. And we charge that none may succour them in their need and distress."

A cage of iron bars was made by the local blacksmith, with rests for their legs and buttocks, and was fixed on the tree beside an old chalk pit now known as Gibbet Pit. Today it supports a clump of beech trees. The two men were seen in their cage by Martha Spigot who was coming home from Yeovil along the old Roman road. They shouted for water: this she did not have but instead she found two tallow candles and pushed them into the mouths of the dying men. But it is said that Martha was caught in the act of helping the doomed men and was herself punished with seven years imprisonment at Dorchester gaol.

The memory of these events has left the landscape with two names—Gibbet Pit and Murderers' Lane. It has also provided the ghost of Thomas Baker who is said to drive along Murderers' Lane with his horse and cart. One old lady, aged ninety in about 1947, described how on a damp and foggy November night in 1865 she walked the lane with her father and mother. All saw Thomas Baker's horse and cart come round a corner, the horse breathing heavily and the wheels of the vehicle creaking, only to vanish in the mist and leave the lane in silence.

The old lady's story was written up by G. W. Greening for the Dorset Year Book of 1949–50.

Netherbury church: don't play with its ghosts.

NETHERBURY

The out-spooked sexton

A CAUTIONARY tale about the inadvisability of playing with ghosts comes from the legend of the white and black spooks in Netherbury churchyard. It was passed down in the family of John Symonds Udal who traced it back to the early part of the nineteenth century.

He was told that the village idiot, "a poor half-witted girl," irritated the sexton—who lived across the wall in a cottage beside the churchyard [Ordnance Survey map reference SY 471 994]—by sitting in the church porch night after night and singing psalms. The sexton decided to frighten her off and wrapped himself in a sheet.

The girl, however, was unsurprised. "Here's a soul coming," she said. "Who's soul be you? Be you my granfer's or granmer's, or be you . . .?" She had named a villager who was recently buried.

"H'm, souls be about tonight," she said as she looked around. "For there's a black 'un too, and he's trying to come up to the whit' 'un; and he's coming on so fast that if the whit' 'un don't take care the black 'un 'll catch en."

It was now the sexton who was in fright and flight, back towards the wall and the safety of home as the girl kept repeating:

"Run, whit' soul; black soul 'll catch 'ee."

The sexton was in severe shock and suffered a severe illness in which his skin peeled from head to foot. The girl continued reciting her psalms in a churchyard that other mortals henceforth avoided at night.

NETHERBURY

A phantom coach-and-four

NORTH BOWOOD dairy farm was anciently a place of significance in the north-west corner of Netherbury parish. Fields at the head of a deep-cut and damp valley cover the sites of a mediaeval mansion house [Ordnance Survey map reference SY 448 997, partly under the present buildings] and a chapel two hundred yards south-west, in the upper fold of the coombe.

It is appropriate that a phantom aristocracy should be serviced by a spectral coach-and-four, which is said to come across the hill from the north-east. There, a mile away at the foot of a steep slope, lies the village of Stoke Abbott. The track over the hill [map reference ST 450 001] is now a public footpath but it was formerly a road. Justice John Symonds Udal, Dorset's foremost collector of folklore, walked it in the last years of the nineteenth century with Major Groves, who told him of the tradition.

NETHERBURY [hamlet of WOOTH]

'The grey lady had usurped my body and mind'

AMANDA ALLSOP, the 24-year-old daughter of author and conservationist Kenneth Allsop of Powerstock, who died in May 1973, went for lunch the following month to Wooth Manor, on the west side of the River Brit between Bridport and Netherbury [Ordnance Survey map reference SY 472 954].

What happened she described for me in her own words whilst the memory was fresh, on 20 October that year:

"I had one of the strangest experiences of my life here. I was visiting the house one day last June with my family and a friend, Liz. The hostess began talking about the presence of a ghost in the house, and Liz mentioned that I had had psychic experiences in the past. I knew nothing about the ghost, or about their conversation; so they approached me, more in fun than in seriousness, to ask if I would look around four particular rooms to see whether I could 'feel' a presence.

"It was a perfect June day, sunny and fresh and clear with no atmosphere of anything eerie or gloomy. We had been sitting outside. The distinctly uncanny air that I felt when we went inside was probably evoked by the fact that I was supposed to be looking for the uncanny.

"I was taken first into the hostess's bedroom, in the middle of the house, and attached to the Gothic wing. I felt the same sense of being obliged to notice something as I had done on entering; so I tried to ignore it. The second room, though, which was a light and sunny guest room, I knew contained a fourth being. The hostess and Liz were with me; but I also knew, as one knows that someone has come into a room and is standing somewhere unseen—behind one's back—that something had come in with us. I couldn't identify it as human or animal, grotesque or attractive. We went on into the third room. Here, the being had arrived before us—as if a person had preceded, not followed, us into the room. Apart from a feeling of slight embarrassment at trying to explain to my friends that there was something else there but that I couldn't say what, I wasn't worried; there was nothing unpleasant about it. I had only a need to justify myself by being more specific.

"In the last room, at the end of the house, the atmosphere and my emotions changed suddenly. This was the same kind of brightly lit and lightly furnished room as the second, and also a guest room. There were no dark peculiar corners to it. But as we went into it I felt a sudden urgency and anxiety. I knew again that something else was with us there. And this time I had to be able to identify it. At the same time as the overwhelming need to identify it hit me, I knew that if I found something I would be able to do so. I began to look. I had no idea what I was looking for or how whatever it was would help me if and when I found it; I only felt extremely agitated and anxious—not panic-stricken. I looked under the bed; behind the curtains; inside the curtained wardrobe; and finally began crawling around the floor on my hands and knees, searching the carpet. I was, at the same time, trying to explain my peculiar behaviour to my friends, who, I thought, must have been feeling as embarrassed by my behaviour as I felt.

"Eventually I gave up. I couldn't find anything, but I still felt certain that there was something to be found in that room. I apologised to my hostess, for my odd behaviour and for my inability to produce any evidence or definition from it.

"She then told me that the figure which existed was that of a lady dressed in grey, her hair in a bun, who had been seen, both in that room and in the first guestroom, anxiously searching for something. They had no idea who she was and had decided that she must be a servant who had perhaps been dismissed for theft and was desperately searching for the missing object to prove her innocence. Other members of the household said she was too well-dressed. Perhaps she was the daughter of the house, who had lost a precious treasured piece of jewellery. Whoever she was and whenever she lived has not been established. I felt only that she had temporarily usurped my body and mind and used me to take on her search for her."

PENTRIDGE [hamlet of WOODYATES]

Monmouth's ghost

James Scott, Duke of Monmouth: his ghost haunted the thatched cottage at Woodyates where he spent his last night of freedom.

TRADITION MAINTAINS that the Duke of Monmouth, during his flight from the battlefield of Sedgemoor which ended in capture near Horton Heath, called at the Woodyates Inn [Ordnance Survey map reference SU 029 194]. The hamlet of Woodyates is on the Roman road from Badbury Rings to Salisbury, lies half-a-mile inside Dorset, and its inn was later called the Shaftesbury Arms. Monmouth was captured early on the morning of 7 July, 1685, eight miles to the south of Woodyates, at a spot now known as Monmouth's Ash [map reference SU 061 072].

The original inn, where the Duke is said to have changed his clothes the previous day, was a thatched cottage on the east side of the main road—not the Georgian building on the opposite side to which the licence was transferred in coaching days. Both buildings have now been demolished. The Shaftesbury Arms was swept away for a road widening scheme in the 1950s.

It was in a room of the old cottage that the Duke was fed on 6 July, 1685, and the following was recorded by Lieutenant Colonel J. Benett-Stanford of Pythouse, Wiltshire, after a visit there in the 1920s:

"I have put down on paper the story I heard from Mrs. Kirby, who was tenant of the place for some years under Lord Shaftesbury. She told me of a ghost that appeared to her in three successive years on 15 July, the day of Monmouth's beheading. Each year she saw a slight light in the bedroom. There was no electric light in the house.

"The ghost was the figure of a tall good-looking young man, well dressed and in a wig, standing in the middle of the room with the light of a summer's night showing through the windows. He stood there for some time and gradually melted away, and on each occasion Mrs. Kirby was disturbed by banging doors.

"Lighting a candle she went out into the passage and found all the bedroom doors open, and as the banging continued below stairs, she went down and found all the indoor doors ajar and swinging. The Kirbys left after the third year, and I believe the house has been empty since."

PIMPERNE

The man from the wardrobe

ON 27 August 1983 one of the residents of Pimperne, a male householder, wrote to me with details of inexplicable happenings. He asked me not to reveal his name or address, in case his children are frightened, and I shall leave his letter on my file of ghost research which will eventually go to the Dorset Record Office:

"As far as I know the house I live in with my wife and two children is an old farm cottage. It has three bedrooms upstairs and the reason I am writing to you is because of one of these rooms.

"We moved into the house just before Christmas 1982, and even then when you walked into this bedroom it felt strange. For a start it always felt colder than the rest of the house even though there is a heater in the room.

"At first me and my wife used the room but things started happening, like the wardrobe started to rattle and at times it felt like something was jumping up and down on the bed.

"We never told the children about this but changed rooms. For a time we had a lodger who we put in the room but while he was there nothing happened. So after he left we decided to put the youngest of our children in the room. As far as we know nothing ever happened from then on. Until, one day, my daughter came up to me and said someone came from her wardrobe every night and read her stories.

"She also said it jumped up and down on the bed and played with her and her toys. On hearing this, because [of] what happened to us, we took her out of the room and closed it up. This was on the 23 August 1983.

"The room was put completely tidy and a chain lock was put on the outside of the door to stop the kids from going in there. On the 24th we all went to Swindon for two days to see my mother-in-law. We came home on the morning of the 27th.

"After being home for about two hours I decided to go into the room and open the window. I went upstairs and slid the chain from the door because it was still locked. I opened the door and was about to walk in when I saw the state of the place. The mattress on the single bed, that my daughter used to sleep on, was half on the floor and the mattress from the double bed was thrown across the room. A Bible which was on the mantelpiece was thrown across the room. All the drawers in the chest of drawers were open and the wardrobe which used to rattle was wide open and all the clothes which were inside were thrown all over the room.

"After seeing this I went to my nextdoor neighbours to see if they had heard anything but they hadn't. The rest of the house was the same as when we left and there was no sign of someone breaking in and besides that as I have already said the room was still locked. I myself believe we have a poltergeist in the room. One point I would like to make is that normally things only happen at night."

New Street, Poole: Rick Burgess saw the ghost in the room behind the middle dormer window.

POOLE

Disturbed by the builders

BUILDING WORKER Rick Burgess disturbed a ghost when he was converting two eighteenth century houses into a fully modernised Georgian style residence on the corner of New Street with Cinnamon Lane in the Old Town at Poole. Rick, aged 27 at the time of the incident in April 1973 and living in Galloway Road, Poole, had never previously experienced anything supernatural. The time of the occurrence was about 9.30 in the evening, when he was working in an attic room behind the centre dormer window of the old house: "I was suddenly aware of a movement out of the corner of my eye. The room we were in was lit, so was the landing a few feet away, and the room opposite. I saw a man disappear from the landing and into the other room. There was no noise, and I didn't see him come upstairs. He seemed to disappear round the corner in one big stride.

"He was wearing a long coat. It could have been a frock coat. It was a tweedy green colour. He had his back to me as I looked. He had long dark hair and it could have been tied back."

Rick's mate, Ian Stewart of Adastral Road, Canford Heath, was the only other person in the building. He saw nothing, but believed his friend's story. "It was the look on Rick's face, a look of incredulity," he was reported as saying in the Evening Echo on 11 May 1973.

The two men went into the room where the man had gone but no one was there. Rick took his wife, Dilys, to the house a couple of nights later: "She is more sensitive over these things and has had one or two experiences with ghosts. She felt nothing in the room where this man disappeared. But there were two rooms downstairs which she said had a definite atmosphere. She stood in one of them and said she felt her flesh creep."

POOLE

Phantom violin

WHEN MR. FRED CALVER, a Poole auctioneer and the owner of a violin, tried to sell the instrument at a sale in January 1966 he did not receive a single bid. Mr. Calver said the 78-year-old instrument had become known as the "Phantom Violin" because his father had returned several times, since his death the previous year, to play it. On the day of the sale Mr. Leonard Connabeer, a former London Philharmonic violinist, played an unnamed air as Mr. Calver opened the proceedings, but no unaccountable noises were heard from the instrument.

Mr. Calver told a correspondent for The Guardian that his wife was too nervous to live in the same house with the instrument which had survived the sinking of the luxury liner *Titanic* on her maiden voyage across the North Atlantic in 1912. "The violin was played by a friend of my father as the ship was sinking. The passengers were singing 'Nearer my God to Thee' and he was the only violinist in the ship's orchestra to survive. The disaster broke his spirit and he gave up playing. My father bought his violin for £20 and it has been in his family ever since."

POOLE

High Street happenings

PSYCHIC NEWS in 1965 and 1966 reprinted several stories from local newspapers concerning inexplicable happenings in Poole High Street. Worried customers, said one report, fled from a shop after seeing objects moving around and the witnesses to the incident included the shop's branch manager. They believed the renewed activity—the shop was also troubled by a poltergeist two years previously—was caused by news that the building would be demolished as part of large scale redevelopment in the High Street area.

Mrs. S. Shaw said that she had seen four Eau de Cologne bottles lifted off a shelf as if by an invisible hand and dropped to the floor in slow motion. Her husband had seen a similar happening with small travelling bags, which were lifted from their hooks, and dropped to the floor. When "Jenkins" last caused a disturbance the Poole and Dorset Herald published accounts from previous tenants who had experienced very similar happenings. The poltergeist had been seen twice.

The next Poole haunting happened at the Crown Hotel, Market Street, in 1966 when the paper described the happenings as the "latest in a long line of local premises to be plagued by poltergeists". A lone note was played on a piano by an invisible hand and there was the sound of a body being dragged across a floor. Later a "fluorescent mist" came down the stairs from the stable towards a group of three witnesses, drifted across the courtyard and out of the hotel entrance. Mr. D. Browne, an Australian staying at the hotel, decided to prove all they had seen was in their imagination.   He painted five crosses on the door, bolted it and went down to the courtyard, then to his horror he saw the door open.   "It was the most eerie feeling I have ever had in my life," he said.   As with the High Street occurrences, it was believed that a ghost had been disturbed.   The landlord, Mr. Alan Brown, said the noises in the stable began when the alterations started to convert the outbuilding into a club for beat music.   Other noises had been heard in the past, including that of a body being dragged across a floor.

PORTLAND

Fabulous sea creature

I HAVE for fifteen years ignored the story of the Portland cock, hoping it would go away, but that seems only to draw attention to its omission.   So here it is, via Raphael Holinshed [died 1590] and John Hutchins:
"In November 1457, in Portland, was seen a cock coming out of the sea having a great crest on its head, a great red beard, and legs half a yard long.   He stood on the water and crowed three times, and every time turned himself about and beckoned with his head, north, south, and west.   He was in colour like a pheasant, and when he had crowed he vanished."
The cock is strongly associated with the Romano-Celtic culture and was the subject of some charming little enamelled brooches, not that I am seriously suggesting a lingering folk memory in this case.   It might more likely have started with the figure-head of a boat being seen after a wreck.   Or, with greater probability, that the entire island population was drunk.

PORTLAND

Shrieks of shipwreck

THE STRANGEST experience of my life took place at about 6 p.m. on Thursday 19 July 1973 just below the highest point on the rocky, barren island of Portland in south Dorset.   On the eastern heights of the island, overlooking the white Dorset cliffs from Ringstead to Purbeck, is Verne Citadel which was built by the Victorians to carry huge gun batteries watching over the approaches to Portland's "harbour of refuge".   The Verne is now a Home Office prison and the other cluster of buildings on the summit of East Weare, the old convict prison at the Grove, has become a Borstal.   The flat top-lands between the twin establishments are eaten into by former Admiralty quarries which provided the stone for the harbour breakwaters.   One column of the original rock strata has been left standing out of the quarry floor, as a navigation mark, and is called Nicodemus Knob.
To the north, a shelf runs out of the seaward corner of the quarry with a track through the tangled bramble undergrowth.   The path disappears [at about Ordnance Survey map reference SY 697 734] into cliffside scree as it reaches the chasm that divides the Verne from the top of Portland.   A wall of rock rises

above this shelf and below are impenetrable thickets that tumble three hundred feet to the sea.

Here on this shelf the phenomena took place. I was walking with a Manchester photographer, Judy Harrison, and we had just taken a picture of Nicodemus Knob in the clear, sharp light of late afternoon for the Royal Naval Association's Portland souvenir magazine. Judy at this time was aged twenty and I was twenty-six. We had walked about a hundred yards along the shelf when we both heard the sounds of waves, wailing and screaming. This continued for about ten seconds and then there was silence.

We continued walking to the great ditch at the south-east corner of Verne Citadel and then went back along the same shelf. On returning and standing at the same point there was for a moment the sound of muted shouting hanging in the air all around us; and as before it was replaced by total silence.

An easy explanation would be that the waves from the rocky beach are echoed to a particular cleft in the uneven rockface but this is not convincing as any sounds of the sea would be continuous. Some noises also drifted up from the dockyard but these were of cars and movement which the brain automatically filters out as being too faint and distant for concern. The difference with the two experiences of inexplicable sound was that they alone saturated the air and our minds for a matter of seconds. They could not be unnoticed or ignored and for both of us speech was impossible whilst they were in progress and relief was instant when they ended. The experience was so real that it could have been a tape-recorded replay of one of Portland's multitude of gruesome shipwrecks. Yet there was no one in sight to trick us, and the way these sounds were unique in our experience was that they did not emanate from a point but filled the air itself.

POWERSTOCK

The terrified Salukis on Eggardon

A NARROW cart-track crosses the exposed top of Dorset's most westerly chalkland escarpment at Eggardon Hill. The unfenced ridgeway runs at 800 feet along the outer rampart of a huge Iron Age fortress and is at the edge of a precipice. Several hundred feet below is the dank and dense woodland canopy of Powerstock Common which with its epiphyte encrusted skeletons of stunted, ancient oaks is one of the few areas of primaeval forest surviving unfelled in southern England.

From the great entrenchments of Eggardon the hill track descends as a narrow lane, deeply cut between tall hedgerows, running to the stone cottages of Powerstock and the lowlands of the Marshwood Vale. The eastern start to this track is at the crossroads near Two Gates where the Roman road across the downs from Dorchester meets with other roads climbing on to the hills from Maiden Newton and Askerswell. Here a white signboard points along Eggardon's track with the words: "Powerstock, West Milton. Unfit for cars."

Over the years there have been frequent stories in Powerstock of horses terrified on this road for no reason, cars and watches stopping, and men's voices calling. The watches and cars are said to have stopped and refused to function again for half-an-hour. The most recent occurrence was reported in Power-stock's parish magazine and said to have happened in the autumn of 1971. The story made it into the Bridport News on 21 January 1972.

It is a story about a Bridport businessman—"un-named but a reliable source tells us he has connections in green grocery and the council chamber," the local paper teased—who drove to Eggardon Hill to exercise his two saluki dogs. These gazelle-hounds were purchased in Arabia and, boasted the owner, "are afraid of nothing".

Usually, that is. On the night in question the businessman stopped at the crossroads with the signpost, to the east of the hill-fort [at Ordnance Survey map reference SY 547 946], and let the animals out of the car: "Immediately they showed signs of fear. They stood, hackles rising, growling at an unseen pheno-menon and were reluctant to leave the car." The walk became impossible so the man went home but he returned on the two following nights with the dogs and a tape recorder as well: "Again the hounds behaved in this strange fashion but a playback later revealed nothing but the moaning of the wind."

The newspaper, seizing on this spooky night and Eggardon's history of strange happenings, asked: "Fact or fantasy? Was Diana, Goddess of the Chase, reputed to haunt the hill, abroad this night? Or is it a case of 'Windy!'"

POYNTINGTON

Civil War battlefield

APPARITIONS ARE to be expected around any battlefield, both as lasting evidence of violent deaths and because the haunting is often a symbolic method of passing on a legend; even a comparatively small flow of blood can stimulate folk memory for generations. One violent affray of the Civil War left an impression so vivid on an isolated Dorset hamlet that the story was perpetuated in local lore for centuries.

Parliamentary soldiers were in June 1644 marching as an organised body towards Wincanton. At the small village of Poyntington, two miles north of Sherborne on the Somerset border, a few royalist sympathisers rallied poorly armed peasants in a rustic revolt to ambush the column. They were led by a frenzied 20-year-old, Baldwin Malet, Esq., who impeached the troops to "halt in the name of the king."

Metal glinted in a meadow by the mill stream [Ordnance Survey map reference ST 653 199] where, dashing horseborne into battle, young Baldwin bravely swept his sword through a score of the foe. Within an hour he was a bloody corpse reposing supine at the house of his father. The ever-present fear of plague followed the swiftness of the decision of battle and the next morning Baldwin was carried to the churchyard. Moist meadow soil was hurriedly used to cover the bodies of the other lifeless combatants of both sides, and these grave mounds can still be seen.

Up to 1870 the memory was so intense that no villager of Poyntington would at night approach the meadow for dread of a ghostly troop of headless men and one decapitated female; her part in the skirmish is not known. The reason for remembering the battle would endure as the fight left a depopulated village which fell to ruin and never returned to its pre-calamity stature.

In the church is an heraldic painting with the arms of the Malet family and the following inscription: "Baldwin Malet, second sonne of Sir Thomas Malet, dyed in the King's service, the 3rd day of Jvne AD 1646 in the Twentieth Yeare of his age."

PUDDLETOWN [hamlet of LOWER WATERSTON]

One century later

ON CHRISTMAS NIGHT, 1862, fire spread through the mediaeval manor house of Waterston, two miles north-east of Puddletown [Ordnance Survey map reference SY 734 952], reducing it to a gutted shell. The stones of the old house were still standing but only one room remained of the original interior, which was rebuilt in Victorian style. Though the fire probably removed the ghost of an eighteenth century girl, who is said to have jumped to her death from an upper window, it created another mystery.

In 1962, Mr. Constantine FitzGibbon, a prolific author, had installed oil-fired central heating and the house was kept well-warmed but they noticed the dining room was growing cold. "The radiators were chilly. I therefore fetched a torch and went to the small cellar under the house where the heating mechanism was. I found that the floor was deep in oil and the furnace red hot," Mr. FitzGibbon wrote in the Daily Telegraph magazine of 22 December, 1967, by which time he had moved to Ireland.

"We waded through hot oil to the control switch and then phoned an engineer at Blandford who came at once. The engineer said that had he not acted immediately, in a matter of minutes the house would have burned: the reason for the leaking oil was that a safety device had inexplicably failed to function, one hundred years later, to the hour."

PURSE CAUNDLE

Fairy plainsong

THE RECORDED reason for pulling out a newel staircase at Purse Caundle manor house was "because of a fairy." Next to it was a well, now covered over, and a "friendly spirit" was said to rise from the well when the ladies of the house climbed the stairs on their way to bed. This troubled the ladies so the ghost was laid with a service of exorcism.

That was late in the last century but stories of the chanting of plainsong and the sound of the hunting horn and cry of hounds at midsummer bring us nearer to the present day.   The hounds are also said to be heard baying on the bowling green on Christmas Eve.   John Aleyn lived on the site of the present manor in 1269 and his duty was to "keep and lodge the King's sick or injured hounds at the King's cost when the Lord King hunts game in Blakemore [the Blackmore Vale]."

These traditions are very fitting for a picturesque country house of yellow stone with steep roofs, gables and mullioned windows.   The house, built about 1470, stands in a small village [Ordnance Survey map reference ST 695 177] four miles east of Sherborne and south from the A30 between Milborne Port and Henstridge.

SANDFORD ORCAS

Hauntings galore

NO CASE of alleged ghostly happenings in Dorset, or indeed anywhere in southern England, aroused more publicity in the second half of the twentieth century than a bizarre series of inexplicable occurrences at Sandford Orcas, a Tudor manor house of yellow Ham stone, three miles north of Sherborne [Ordnance Survey map reference ST 623 210].   Colonel and Mrs. Francis Claridge, who were leasing the manor from the Medlycott family, invited a team of three researchers from the Paraphysical Laboratory to spend a night at the house in 1966.   Mr. Benson Herbert, who led the team, said "there is a prima facie case for the house being haunted."

Earlier that year Mrs. Claridge encountered an elderly woman in a red dress, who made her way upstairs from the great hall and disappeared into the solarium, without opening the door.   The woman is believed to be the grandmother of one of the people who lived at the manor a century ago.   Once the Claridges' son-in-law, John, was awakened on a moonlit night between 2 and 4 a.m. and looked out from the window to see a woman in Elizabethan dress, with a high collar, walk from the manor towards the courtyard and then disappear.   On another occasion Colonel Claridge was showing two women around the house when a man in modern dress entered the great hall.   He was seen by Mrs. Claridge and recognised as Sir Hubert Medlycott who was portrayed in a picture which was at one time kept in the house.

Another male ghost at the manor was said to have been caught in a snapshot taken in the grounds: the figure of a man dressed in a white shepherd's smock appears in a photograph taken in July 1966 at about 3.30 in the afternoon.   No one was seen when the picture was taken but on being developed it showed the figure clearly standing beside a wall.   "This man is probably one of two farmers who lived in the house for a period of 120 years: he often appears passing the kitchen windows between 3 and 4 p.m., no doubt coming in just before or after milking," said Colonel Claridge.

From the time the colonel and his wife moved into the manor early in 1965 they claimed to have heard beautiful music, as if someone was playing a harpsichord or spinet, carried in the air from a room over the arched gatehouse above the drive at the entrance to their home.   Voices were heard, the Claridges said, and people walked about in various parts of the house. Furniture and a picture had moved and a window was often found to have opened itself.

On 16 December 1966 the Western Gazette published a letter from Mr. Anthony Medlycott of Edmonsham House, Cranborne, writing partly on behalf of his son, the present owner of the house. Mr. Medlycott had been angered by a recent BBC programme on ghosts at Sandford Orcas and wrote: "During living memory the house has been lived in by members of my family continuously from 1916 till 1964. During the whole of that time no ghosts were seen nor were any unusual sounds or happenings noticed by either the family or their guests or staff. Had there in fact been any tales of ghosts (I myself am no disbeliever in ghosts) there would have been no reason to suppress them, though doubtlessly they would not have been communicated to the press, nor would there have been any public spooking."

Colonel Claridge replied that he had letters, entirely unsolicited, from people who had worked for the late Sir Hubert Medlycott, testifying to the fact of their having seen apparitions. He also claimed to have a testimony from a man who lived there in 1903, some years before the Medlycott family inherited the property. Two others who had experiences in the house many years ago told their stories to the Evening Echo, Bournemouth.

The first was Miss M. Gallo, aged 17, of Hinton Admiral, who wrote: "I lived there with my parents who worked at the house for $3\frac{1}{2}$ years. I was six years old and my sister was five. We heard knocking on the doors, windows opening and closing, and curtains being drawn backwards and forwards. At the time, my parents didn't believe us, as we were small."

Mrs. J. N. Grange-Bennett of Horseshoe Cottage, Brudenell Avenue, Poole, was born at Sandford Orcas, as was her sister, the old manor being their parents' home for several years. "My mother," she wrote, "always told me that the house was haunted. At night, bells would ring, upstairs windows would open and foot-steps were often heard on the stone staircase leading to the bedrooms. My mother's small terrier, which slept at the foot of a four-poster bed, would become almost hysterical, growling and barking, apparently at some unseen presence."

The village hit back against this stream of recollections and multiple hauntings with a professionally painted traffic hazard sign, using red and black lettering on a white background, which appeared on a tree beside the lane at Christmas in 1966: "Caution. Ghosts 100 yards."

My personal credulity was stretched to snap-point in 1973–74, by which time the national press at Christmas was depending upon 63-year-old Colonel Francis Claridge for its seasonal ghostly enlivening. A phone call from London to the manor house at Sandford Orcas would produce useable haunting quotes. For instance: "This place comes alive with them [ghosts] when visitors are here. Scores of guests have been forced to flee." And the Colonel's wife reported similar experiences: "The bad one from the back part has been about again this week. The evil one in the nursery wing, where nobody can sleep, he's walking about."

Their daughter, Anne Claridge, claimed 22 ghosts in the building and "umpteen round the grounds." She had seen seventeen. The Claridges welcomed television cameras and the Colonel's wife wrote on 7 November 1966: "I do not object to publicity as we are anxious to make the place of public interest so as to further our desire to build a Cancer Research laboratory here."

This was the point made by a 'notice' published from the manor in 1965: "It is proposed this summer to open a laboratory for Cancer Research on the premises with a resident anilitical [sic] chemist. All monies collected will be devoted to research work and the maintenance of the property. Your generous contributions will be gratefully received and acknowledged. Please make payable to Colonel F. Claridge."

By 1970 the spooks had multiplied from the original mere handful. In 1973 the Ghost Club decided to investigate and hired a coach from London. The club was founded in 1862 with Charles Dickens among its first members, and had as its chairman Tom Perrott who studied the emergence of the Sandford Orcas phenomena in the mid-1960s when he was secretary of the Society of Dorset Men.

The coach party failed to meet a ghost but the afternoon was unprecedented for sheer entertainment value. Colonel Claridge invited the first group of a dozen into his house, told them it was built in 1042 (an exaggeration of four centuries), and turned to one of the ladies: "No photographs indoors. We've been burgled, that's why we don't allow it."

The party was swept through the first three rooms, casually shown pewter, Hogarth engravings, and a miscellany of antiques with an uninterrupted flow of gripping Claridge descriptions: "And this is a seventeenth century Mandarin's judgment chair. They would sit there and decide whether you could keep your head. If not, they used to have it off straight away."

All the time the Colonel's hearing aid screeched: "There's a bit of damp about today and if I turn it down I can't hear. So it's going to keep whistling—it's not the ghosts!" These were announced in an upstairs room. "Now you want to hear about the ruddy ghosts I suppose," Claridge said. "There were two juicy murders in this room. One was a Moorish servant strangled by the wire you cut cheese with—can you feel it on your neck? The other was a priest who smothered his master."

One morning at four o'clock the Colonel was woken with the feel of a monk's habit coming down over his face—"so I stopped that one with a crucifix." But the Moor still makes yearly visits: "He will come back next week, every night at 2 a.m. for seven days, and then we won't be troubled with him again for a year."

The Colonel continued: "There are three cowled monks at 7.30 a.m. I was so surprised I called my wife's attention to it and three more monks came. They were celebrating the feast of St. Francis. Interesting, isn't it?"

"Yes, very interesting," the females in his audience duly chorused. In the next room the bed was the scene of two murders: "One gentleman came here and saw the whole murder. He couldn't face any more and wouldn't go any further around the house. Some people see it, and others don't. It depends whether you are lucky.

"Between ten and eleven a very nice man comes down tapping five times and then seven times up, and my daughter won't come into the house after dark."

The best story came last. Colonel Claridge told the Ghost Club of a naval cadet who entered Dartmouth College at the age of 14, but within two years was back in the house as a prisoner after he had killed a boy. "There was a story that he was a sex maniac, but I don't believe it as when the moon was full he was allowed to walk around the village. They don't let sex maniacs out at any time. I didn't believe that twaddle. Yet he was kept there from new moon to full moon until he was a raving man and died aged 27 years.

"He's buried in the passage behind my bed!"

Gasps, then the Colonel carried on with his lecture: "You know that women always dote over their youngest child, because it is their last effort. An old butler came here and said his mistress never went near the passage when John was alive; but then she went every day.

"He's in there, plastered from behind to keep the smell of mortified flesh out."

This must have happened a long time ago, someone remarked. "He died in 1947," the Colonel answered. Astonishment. Mutterings all round with one lady saying: "That's the year I got married."

"I've got a very long lease of this, signed before I knew about the ghosts," said the Colonel as he firmly changed the subject back to antiques and his weapons of execution.

The owner of Sandford Orcas manor house, baronet Sir Christopher Medlycott of Milborne Port, confirmed that the Colonel had a lease until 1979: "I don't believe it is haunted at all, as we lived there for 44 years and never heard anything. He's been there since April 1965 and I am sorry to disillusion you but nobody believes it's haunted except him. It's absolutely fatuous, the stories he tells."

I then gave Sir Christopher an account of the walled-up naval cadet: "What! But that's ridiculous, that's absolutely ridiculous. My parents were living there at the time. No such things happened. It's absolute lies."

The John to whom the Colonel referred could only be John Hubert Nicholas Medlycott, Sir Christopher's younger brother, who died unmarried aged 27 on 22 February, 1948. However he died in Northampton of bronchial pneumonia.

Jackie Gillot, the author and broadcaster who lived at Bruton, told me she had met the Colonel: "We strolled into the walled garden and a strange figure in shorts came across from the top with the sound wee, wee, wee. This figure said, 'I'd like eight bob off you lovelies, wee, wee, wee.' I then realised he had terrible feedback [from the hearing aid] which he was too deaf to notice.

"Then we were taken on the tour of the house. Once he got into the bedroom he got more excited, pushing me around with his stomach and winking and blinking, saying things like: 'Don't you think that's a good bed. Feel it, I got it out of a Spanish nunnery.'

"'And now something to really interest you—ghosts!' He showed us a photograph and said 'there's a Franciscan monk, there's a mediaeval farmer, there's an Elizabethan woman.' I said, I can't see a thing. 'Can't see a thing, hang on and I'll get a magnifying glass.' They were badly taken, blurred photographs and I was the first person not to see anything in them."

Deric James, the Bournemouth editor of an occult magazine, Insight, spent a night at the house: "We took tape recorders and infra-red cameras but the only sounds we picked up were knocking, ringing of bells and a thump. It had been a very hot day and the night was so cold it could easily have been the contracting of the house. The bells sounded like Swiss cowbells but we only heard them for about seven or eight seconds. The only thing that happened was about six o'clock in the morning when there was the apparent shape of a dog that appeared.

"The reporters were genuinely alarmed. But you get one suggestion from someone that they've seen something and, although three other people claimed to have seen it from different places, I think it was all a case of auto-suggestion. I didn't believe it.

"The noises came from the nursery wing which the Colonel said was inaccessible. He could only get there by scaling the roofs and walls.   Besides, the Colonel and his wife live there on their own; why should he do it?

"We were locked in all night and the Colonel didn't let us out until 10 o'clock the next morning. Some of us had to get back to Bournemouth early so we started banging on the door about eight but he never came. Some time later, I heard he'd been showing a party round and in the course of his talk mentioned how we'd spent the night there and had been so frightened we'd been banging on the door to get out! It was all nonsense of course."

By 1974, after nine years of following the Sandford Orcas ghostly hordes, Tom Perrott became another disillusioned sceptic. When he read Jane Claridge's latest claims in Psychic News he commented: "I think she must be suffering from multiple spectreosis." Perrott, in 1966, sent a donation to the cancer project but in the following years he heard nothing of its progress. Initially, Perrott so much wanted to believe in the ghosts of Sandford Orcas, yet even his credulity had suffered a jolt when he led his Ghost Club out from the manor. To add to his disappointment, the Colonel refused to accept Perrott's cheque, saying something about his "bank being abroad".

Along the stairway in the house, one visitor had admired a small etching of Ven House at Milborne Port, and said "we passed that in the coach". This prompted Perrott to ask Colonel Claridge about the large painting of Ven, hanging in the Solarium at Sandford Orcas, which had fallen down one night. On 13 February 1967, the Colonel told Benson Herbert of the Paraphysical Laboratory that he had found the picture "previously hanging on the wall of the solar room" standing on the floor against a chair "some eight feet from the wall and with a corner broken". This had happened often, though up to then without damage.

At the time of the 1973 visit, this incident escaped the Colonel's memory and only after Perrott's initial exasperation—"don't you remember?"—had turned into a minutiae of recollections did the Colonel's memory recover: "By poltergeists, yes. We've got that room chained up now." One of the party was verbally unconvinced "That was last week!"

For all the incredibility, the Colonel was still good copy for book writers and James Turner, in a 1973 ghostly effort from David and Charles, Ghosts in the South West, put into print the man's every word with only a gentle hint of possible reservations: "I came away from the house saturated with psychic wonders. If all these phenomena did occur, the house must indeed be the most haunted in the West Country." Turner, with a good eye for a story, did not spoil his book by doing anything investigative like phoning Sir Christopher Medlycott. His single bright suggestion was that Colonel and Mrs. Claridge might themselves be ghosts: "So saturated was I with 'happenings' that it would not have surprised me if they, too, had melted away."

That was prophetic. For subsequently the Claridges left their ghosts and the house was reoccupied by Medlycotts.

Just one of the ghosts at Sandford Orcas: an Elizabethan gentleman in neck-ruff, drawn by Philip Edon of RAF Linholme, Doncaster, who met the figure in April 1972.

The brown monk

THE RUINS of Shaftesbury Abbey remain a memorial to the Convent of St. Edward, a nunnery of the Benedictine order, who were in continuous occupation of the hilltop between the reigns of King Alfred and Henry VIII. With the piles of stones, foundations, floors and coffins of the past lives a spirit who protects a secret of hidden riches buried shortly before the dissolution. The legend says this monk, who is still seen in his brown habit, was commanded by the last Abbess, Elizabeth Souche, to choose a suitable site beneath the ground and with blindfolded workmen excavate a pit to receive the silver plate and gold treasures of the Abbey [Ordnance Survey map reference ST 862 229]. The task of furnishing the secret chamber completed, the monk went with its key to the Abbess but before he could disclose the whereabouts, he had a stroke and died.

Excavations in 1932 failed to uncover his secret and, though diviners say there is gold under the eight hundred feet hill that is Shaftesbury, it has never been found. The appearance of the monk has created one of the best-known ghostly occurrences in Dorset and he has often been seen hurrying along the outer walk and disappearing through the wall at a point where once there must have been an entrance. Because he is visible from the knees upwards it is presumed that the level of the ground was lower in his time.

In the days of the curfew, subterranean passages were built under the hill so that, in a case of great illness, a priest could be summoned to attend a nun in the Abbey. It is along these tunnels that the monk travels and he has appeared in various parts of ancient Shaftesbury.

*   *   *   *   *

Two Tudor men leading packhorses were seen on Gold Hill, by friends of Marion Wright in 1965, and it was up these steep cobbles that a ghostly cavalcade of horsemen has risen. This procession is said to be the funeral cortège of the young King Edward who was stabbed in the back at Corfe Castle—knifed by a servant of his stepmother, Elfthryth. In the words of William of Malmsbury: "The Kinge, findeing himselfe hurt, sette spurs to his horse, thinking to recover his companie; but the wounde beeing deepe, and fainting through the losse of much blood, he fell from his horse, which dragged him by one foot hanging in the stirrop, untill he was left dead at Corfe gate, Anno Dom. 979."

The body is said to have been found later, in an uncorrupted state, "by warning from heaven" and miracles happened whilst it was being carried to Shaftesbury, where the king became Saint Edward the Martyr. The corpse was entombed on the north side of the principal altar on 12 March 980 and his shrine was uncovered by the digging before the war. Relics, supposed to be of the boy king, used to be displayed in the abbey grounds but then languished in a bank vault whilst ownership was disputed. Among those said to have heard the clattering of the ghostly cavalcade was Kenneth Horne [of "Round the Horne" fame in the last great days of steam wireless] who had no previous knowledge of the phenomenon.

Nine o'clock Albert

ALBERT, THE punctual poltergeist of St. Anthony's cottage at Butts Knapp, Shaftesbury, made an appearance in the London Evening News of 22 February 1966. He was sharing the house with "two pretty girl secretaries", 26-year-old Miss Judith Atkinson and 24-year-old Miss Hazel Wright. "We now take Albert for granted," Judith said, "although some of his tricks can be a little upsetting."

The time that Albert chose for making himself known was nine o'clock in the evening. "Locked doors open and shut, lights flash on and off, footsteps echo through the house and mysterious shadows come and go," the newspaper reported. Once there was misbehaviour away from the regular slot when, Judith said, "we heard screams in the night." The police were told but found nothing.

Another time Hazel felt a prod in the back when she was washing her hair and no one else was in the room.

The pranks had been going on for a year and were a topic of conversation around which social life could revolve. Friends had been invited to the house to listen to him and try to solve the mystery. "Albert seems too friendly to call in professional ghost hunters to stop his activities," Hazel said. "As long as he behaves himself we're quite willing to put up with him."

SHERBORNE

Sir Walter Raleigh

"THAT WHOSOEVER shall take those lands from the bishopric, or diminish them, in great or small, should be accursed, not only in this world, but also in the world to come; unless in his lifetime he made restitution thereof." With that curse Osmond, Bishop of Sarum, gave his lands at Sherborne to the church.

The estates around Sherborne [Old] Castle remained the property of the Bishop of Salisbury until King Stephen took them away, at which time his prosperity ended and the lands went to the Montague family, who lost their male line. The property was restored to the church, next to be taken by the Duke of Somerset, who shortly after was called to London and decapitated. Queen Elizabeth later misappropriated the estate—she gave it in 1592 to Sir Walter Raleigh, her favourite seaman patriot.

"The fatality attending the unjust purchasers of this demesne has been ascribed to the strange curse attached to Sherborne Castle," it has been said, and for Raleigh the sunset began in 1603 with James's accession. Called by the Attorney General a traitor, monster, viper, and spider of hell, Raleigh was thrown into the Tower of London, but he was still a popular hero and his passage to the block was delayed until 29 October 1618 when he was beheaded by two blows at the age of sixty-eight.

Raleigh found the only peace of his life during his short "retirement" at

Sherborne [New] Castle [Ordnance Survey map reference ST 649 164] and it is in the quiet setting of his arbour, in the lake-side pleasure grounds, that he is said to appear each year on the eve of the feast of St. Michael [29 September].   After walking peacefully under the trees he sits below Raleigh's oak and then vanishes.

Following the execution of Raleigh, the estate went to Prince Henry "who died not long after the possession thereof" and from him to the Earl of Somerset who "lost them, and many other greater fortunes".   After being credited with so much despair the curse must have been satiated as the land came into the hands of the Digby family who hold it still.

**Sir Walter Raleigh's
seat in Sherborne Park,
where he used to have a quiet smoke.**

SHIPTON GORGE/BURTON BRADSTOCK

The Bottom full of ghosts

THE LANE from Shipton Gorge to Burton Bradstock crosses the parish boundary in The Bottom—as the locals call it—where trackways branch off to the east and west.   On the map the spot is called St. Catherine's Cross [Ordnance Survey map reference SY 496 907].

Traditions from both parishes associate it with suicide burials and a cacophony of ghosts.   When I interviewed Mrs. Muriel Aylott in 1969 for her 1920s memories of Shipton Gorge folklore she told me that a spectral coach was amongst them, chased by a baying but headless dog:

"Anyway, this particular one, there was a coach and horses accompanied by four headless men and on a moonlight night they pass from one hedge to another and, I believe this is where the dog came in, chased by a headless dog.   The farm people, the older people there, they would avoid going there at twelve o'clock at night, midnight, on a moonlit night, but later on people said it was the moon shining through the trees, you see, and the creaking of the trees.   In those days they were full of superstition and if one man could tell a story that would scare the other one, then they were pleased with it.

"I know that several groups of people have been there on a particularly moonlit night, at twelve o'clock, but they've never seen anything."

Mrs. Aylott's daughter added that when they lived at Shipton Gorge the villagers believed The Bottom was full of ghosts:

"I used to live there too, you see, and as a child we were warned that there were ghosts in The Bottom.   This is what we called it, you know, The Bottom, at the bottom of the hill.   We didn't think anything of it but it might have been in the whole village and passed down from generation to generation, you see, and we think that our generation were told about the ghosts just to frighten us.   To make sure that we didn't go too far out of the village."

There may well be something in this, as The Bottom coincides with the parish boundary and one of the purposes of the ancient beating-the-bounds ceremonies was to impress upon young children precisely how far they could go without venturing into danger—or coming home to a thrashing.

SILTON

**Silton church:
venue for meeting
a phantom priest.**

Fully vested priest

SEVERAL PEOPLE are said to have seen the phantom priest of Silton church [Ordnance Survey map reference ST 783 294], according to local historian Doris Moore of Bourton. The figure is fully vested and comes towards the altar, and then slides from the chancel into the vestry. This part of the church is an ancient chantry from which there is no exit; the roof has fine fan-vaulting and some angels are painted on the wall above the communion table.

Sometimes they can be seen—but on other days the angels are said to be there no longer. Silton is a tiny village between Gillingham and Bourton in the most northerly extremity of Dorset.

SPETISBURY

Ghost rider in the snows

RENDEZVOUS LODGE was two miles from the nearest tarred road and as isolated as any building in Dorset. It stood in the belt of trees on the downs west of Spetisbury, a few yards off the dirt track that was formerly the turnpiked coach road over the hills from Wareham to Blandford, and was on the Ordnance Survey map from 1811 to 1970 [reference ST 886 008]. That, virtually, was the span of its existence. It must have been built in the first decade of the nineteenth century and its demolition took place in 1966. When I searched for it I arrived a year too late and it was a pile of red brick and roof rafters lying at the edge of a former clearing that had been largely won back by the wood over the past decades. A well lay just beyond the foundations.

Gnarled old fruit trees were in bud and the daffodils were in flower across the former kitchen garden. "Pretty, but it's a frightening place to be alone," said a log-man who came up on me from a rusty pick-up truck. "In the snows I heard a scooter go along the track but it was blocked and there were no marks. I think of it as the ghostly schoolteacher. They laugh at me, but they'd never have the nerve to come here themselves. It all happened this time of year, in the evening."

The events he outlined were the bizarre suicide in the derelict lodge of a 30-year-old Hamworthy pottery teacher who tricked a 16-year-old schoolgirl into shooting him through the chest. He had set up a photographic session with her as the model. She was talked into posing with a handgun and pointing it at him. He reassured her that it was only loaded with blanks and said he needed the smoky effect of the gun being fired. He had her stand astride above him with the gun being aimed at his stomach as he lay flat on the floor with the camera. She was told to close her eyes and fire the gun. It went off once but she was told to keep pulling the trigger or the picture would be spoilt.

After the third shot she opened her eyes and looked down in horror as blood soaked his shirt and oozed from his mouth.

It all seemed too much to believe but later I searched out the newspaper cuttings of the event. Its date was 14 April 1965. The coroner, M. L. Bailey, said at the inquest that this was a case where truth was indeed stranger than fiction. John Downey, a talented and apparently cheerful, healthy young man had concealed a peculiar and unnatural obsession about revolvers and pointed weapons. He had an urge to have pain inflicted upon his stomach. He dearly loved the girl he had tricked but, the inquest heard, she had known him a long time and had no reason to think that he would deceive her. His behaviour towards her had always been correct and he had never done anything to harm her physically in any way: "He staged his own death through the guiltless hands of this young girl."

John Downey ensured that no one could ever think she was other than a totally innocent participant in his morbid scheme. He left a two page letter that was meticulous in its detail:

"This letter is to state that Miss Lyndsey Elaine Riggs, of 48 Kingston Road, Poole, Dorset, is completely innocent of my death by shooting. Although her finger will pull the trigger and send the bullets into me she thinks that she is actually only using *blanks* [his emphasis]!

"I have told Miss Riggs that the bullets are only blanks and that they will not harm me, and that I want a photograph of the muzzle flashes from a gun pointed at me.*

"Miss Riggs, not knowing much about guns and nothing about bullets and ammunition, has believed me. In writing this letter I am not giving any excuses for my actions, and the dreadful thing that I am making Miss Riggs do. I am writing this letter so that you will *not* condemn her of a crime she is *not* guilty of.

"I chose the old house as a good place of execution, as it is too far for anyone to hear the shots.

"I hope that this letter will clear Miss Lyndsey Riggs's name and that she will be clear of any charges made against her in connection with my shooting as *I* alone have tricked her into doing this, and I hope she will soon get over the shock. Although you may not believe me, I am very fond of her. In fact, I love her dearly.

John L[eonard] Downey

* [Footnote, in capital letters.] "I told Miss Riggs that a woman would pay a large sum of money for a picture of a gun being fired using blanks. This she believed I am afraid. It was the only way I could get her to shoot me."

STALBRIDGE

Enveloped in flames

SOME YEARS before the manor house was demolished at Stalbridge Park [Ordnance Survey map reference ST 732 181], strange tales spread in the north Dorset market town, concerning the month when the old building was left in the care of an elderly housekeeper. It was at Christmas and the owner of the house had lent the building to a friend, on the condition that the housekeeper was to remain in charge.

This woman asked the visiting family to make a point of not being in the main hall at five o'clock of an evening. Her request was observed but one day the lady lost count of time and was in the hall at the hour of five, when a figure came from a first floor bedroom door—it was that of a woman enveloped in flames—muttering to herself: "I have done it." As the figure disappeared into the next room, the lady followed to the top of the stairs and found the doors of both rooms were locked. When next evening the same thing happened, the lady gathered together her children and left for London.

On contacting the owner of the house, she was told that it had once been occupied by a widowed mother and her son. One day the boy told his mother he was going to marry the gamekeeper's daughter and that, despite her objections, she should accept the inevitable. For some months, the son and his bride were not allowed to enter the house, but then the mother apparently had a change of heart and invited the couple to live with her. One evening, the son returned late from hunting and was told his wife had burnt to death. She had entered her mother-in-law's dressing room at about five o'clock, changed ready for dinner, and sat beside the fire as the other woman was before her looking glass. There was a scream and the widow turned to see the girl enveloped in flames, having trailed her long dress in the hearth. The story was accepted without question and not until her death-bed did the old lady confess to her son that she had pushed his wife into the fire. After the death of the murderess, the old house was haunted by her figure, surrounded by flames and exclaiming her own guilt.

The ghost was laid with the pulling down of the house in 1822. The most eminent of those who lived at the old manor was the Hon. Robert Boyle who began his chemical experiments there in 1646.

STEEPLE [hamlet of CREECH GRANGE]

Phantom army

A CLASSIC among Dorset ghost stories is that recorded by Rev. John Hutchins, the county historian, who states that in December 1678, horsemen brought a message to London that an army of several thousands had landed on a hilly part of the South Coast. The armed men were marching with a clash of weapons along the Purbeck ridgeway above the mansion of Creech Grange [Ordnance Survey map reference SY 910 817]; ministers forgot Christmas and hastily prepared to muster their forces to meet the invader.

The army was seen by Captain John Lawrence, the respected owner of the Grange, and many of his tenant cottagers left their suppers cooking on the fire and fled to alarm the town of Wareham, four miles to the north. Panic spread through the town and boats at anchor were drawn to the safety of the north bank of the River Frome which divides the anciently walled town from Purbeck. Townsmen barricaded Wareham's narrow South Bridge over the river, as three hundred militia were marched as reinforcements. Everyone waited for the siege.

To London sped Lawrence who deposed particulars of the army on oath before the Privy Council, and war nerves returned to the capital that little wanted to defend its Stuart crown.   The fight to overthrow the tyranny of the Stuart monarchy was not to come till the following decade when James, Duke of Monmouth mismanaged his rebellion and William of Orange came in 1688 to finish the job and dethrone with regal style.   The army that caused the scare of 1678 was hidden in the falling of night and when dawn uncovered the hills it had vanished.   It was a ghost!

Did the phenomenon of a phantom army happen, or was it a vision created by the sea mist and twisted to reality by minds believing their expectancy of invasion had been fulfilled?   Lawrence was recalled to London for his explanation. The known "affection" he held for the regime spared him severe punishment, yet his account of the clash of arms is still dubious, for having once sworn truth to the tale of Dorset countrymen, he could not later retract and say he was beguiled by the weather.

A feasible explanation was given to me by my not-so-old English teacher from Bournemouth, David Popham, who thought he had seen the apparition.   "The mist curled and combed over the dips of the hill and it looked as if a long cloud of dust was being thrown up by a line of people marching.   It is now unusual to find any number of people walking along a dirt road, but had this been the seventeenth century, I could easily have taken it for the advance guard of an army.   The tracks would then have been of trodden chalk dust, and I know that a flock of sheep can be visible for miles by the cloud rising from its path.   Armies on the move would therefore produce the same effect."

I find this answer is only acceptable if the Dorset countrymen of 1678 are assumed to have been stupid.   Certainly they were ignorant and superstitious in many ways, but definitely not about the weather which was such a controlling factor over daily life, and of which they had considerable knowledge, as is clearly shown by the generations of lore that had been accumulated.   This makes it more difficult to believe that the sea mist, which falls strangely so often in Purbeck, could deceive them into imagining a column of marching men.

*   *   *   *   *

The ghost army of Purbeck has a longer pedigree and is said to be of Roman soldiers, who leave the Worbarrow Bay clifftop fortress of Flower's Barrow, and march along Bindon Hill above Lulworth Cove, especially when the current world is at war.   People say it exists, or that it is possible to uncomfortably feel an inexplicable presence.   The thud of the trampling of horses and men is plainly heard and their indistinct forms seen as the fog drifts; "on those nights no rabbits and no dog can be induced to go near."

If ghosts exist, then it is obvious that soldiers who died for the futile causes of kings have every reason to haunt the scene of their pointless slaughter.   It is interesting that the Purbeck case does not coincide with the place of an actual battle, unless this was at the time of the Roman invasion between A.D. 43–47 when the Iron Age hill fort of Flower's Barrow—one of the stronger earthworks with double ramparts sited in an ideal strategic position—was probably one of more than twenty *oppida* violently stormed by Vespasian's Second Legion (Augusta).   Only excavation on a massive scale could uncover the secrets of the majestic fort, poised 550 feet above the beach at Worbarrow Bay, but this is extremely unlikely while the vast ancient monument is part of a Ministry of Defence tank gunnery range.

STINSFORD [hamlet of HIGHER BOCKHAMPTON]

Figure of Rome

DORSET COUNTY COUNCIL owns a public picnic area at Thorncombe Wood, a short distance from Thomas Hardy's birthplace at Higher Bockhampton, to the east of Dorchester. There, in October 1969, no less than fourteen people made the first modern sighting of the ghost of a Roman soldier in Dorset.

A party of a dozen Borstal boys from Guy's Marsh at Shaftesbury were on a "working camp" in the wood with two adults. At about 8.30 on the evening of 13 October a boy rushed into the staff caravan to say there was a ghost among the trees near the camp. The officer thought it was a practical joke and took little interest but the boy was insistent and obviously shaken. So the man left the caravan.

There, thirty yards away, was the figure of a Roman soldier complete with shield, sword, toga and helmet. He was standing in the air "about two feet off the ground." The staff man went back to the caravan for a strong torch and then, with the boys, he approached the figure which promptly disappeared.

Later checking confirmed that the camp was almost exactly on the line of the old Roman road from Dorchester to Badbury Rings [Ordnance Survey map reference SY 727 920]. The significance of the Roman being seen suspended in the air was that he was standing on the level of the road as it was when originally constructed in the first century A.D.

STOURPAINE

Drowned for a wager

BEFORE THE introduction of traffic lights to control the junction of the A357 with the A350 at Durweston Bridge [Ordnance Survey map reference ST 864 086] it was a monthly occurrence for another lorry driver to push part of the newly repaired greensand parapet back into the River Stour. Invariably the damage was done to the south-east side of the bridge, facing the oaks on the east bank of the river in the parish of Stourpaine. "No doubt you saw the horsemen," villagers would joke on the rare occasions when it was a local man who had done the damage.

Mrs. Mary E. Bradley explained the tradition for me in 1968: "Years ago two horsemen made a wager; who would first reach Durweston Bridge from Blandford. They were galloping neck and neck and so fast that they could not pull up on arrival at the bridge.

"As a result the horses jumped the parapet and were killed instantly. The riders also drowned in the river. It is said you can see a rider, or both riders, under the oaks. I have been there on foot and in all sorts of vehicles, at all hours of the day and night. I've never seen or heard a sound to suggest a ghost, so this is imagination arising out of fact."

Cottage in flames

AN OLD woman living in Studland in the middle of the nineteenth century graphi-
cally described a ghost story associated with a cottage in the village. A smuggler
with bales of silk was supposed to have been murdered at the cottage, and from a
distance at sea from on board ship, the cottage appeared to be always in flames
until the rector of the parish was summoned to exorcise the spirit.

The story was passed on to Justice John Symonds Udal by Albert Bankes of
Wolferton who said that the woman it had come from was still alive in about
1856.

The phantom donkey

CLOSE TO midnight on 22 December 1929 a Purbeck fisherman, Ben Pond, was
walking across the northern fringes of the great Studland Heath, from his boat at
Shell Bay to the clay company shack at Goathorn where he lived. In 1969 he
recalled for the Dorset County Magazine:

"No one lived within miles of the track I had to take, nor were there any roads.
I had only a ten-inch wide path trodden by wild cows when walking in single
file. These cows had escaped from distant crofts in years gone by.

"This path, being of peat, would be almost black in colour and bordered by
tall clumps of heather and brushwood. Being young and fit I thought nothing of
doing this four-mile walk, at least until a certain night—22 December.

"That night I had moored my boat at Shell Bay at a late hour, somewhere about
11.30, and then begun my lonely walk. I had gone nearly one and a half miles
when I saw a white object about 100 yards ahead, right in my path. I stopped; it
must be a sheet of newspaper perhaps, but I was a bit scared. How did it get
there? There was no wind, yet it moved, but only slightly. By now I was really
afraid.

"I could not go on. It moved again. Then I decided to get into the heather
and make a big half-circle to avoid the object and so regain the path further on.
This I did. When I had gone about halfway I dared to look at the 'thing,' and
now I could see it broadside on, not end on as at first.

"It was only a white donkey—but wait.

"Now laughing at my fears, I regained the track and looked back. Yes, there it
stood, a white innocent donkey, or was it? Then suddenly it was gone, a
complete disappearance. It was no more.

"Again I was filled with doubts and fears; surely it could not have reached a
clump of bushes sixty yards away and near to Bramble Bush Bay [the inlet at
Ordnance Survey map reference SZ 031 858]. Nor was it just a sheet of paper as I
had first imagined; perhaps that idea had come to mind in thinking back to a
night when someone had suspended long sheets of white paper in Poole cemetery

and some nearby residents were afraid to leave their homes for quite a time.

"I hurried home. Surely, if I returned that way in daylight, I should find hoof marks on the soft peat and patches of sand. But next day when I came back to the spot there were none, not even one hoof print. No, never again would I tread this path by night, I would take the shore route instead. I made this vow after certain facts came to light."

Ben Pond asked the crofters at the foot of Ballard Down, and on the other side of the great heath towards Corfe Castle, if they knew of anyone who had allowed a white donkey to roam the heath. But of more than forty donkeys in the area, none was white. It was not until a few months later, when he was talking to another fisherman, Jim Coffin, in the Bankes Arms at Studland, that he met another person who had seen the white donkey. Coffin gave a very odd look and said in a low voice: "I too have seen that same donkey, 'tis there three days afore Christmas. I knows as I came the heath way meself. Was I afrightened? Not arf!"

Old Coffin continued: "You know old man Marsh, comes from Branksome to pick winkles and dig a bit o' bait; did sometimes sleep on Shell Bay side o' Harbour to be ready for early morn low tide. 'E too did see this donkey. So did some o' Riggs gang when they went to hide a load o' rum in Little Sea sedges.

"Back along 160 years agone, a feller was riding a white donkey three nights afore Christmas near Bramble Bush Bay when he was set on and murdered by a navy deserter who took the bag of money and cask o' rum the poor feller had. The donkey ran away."

STURMINSTER NEWTON

A torpedoed ghost story

OLIVE KNOTT was very disappointed, in 1973, when I told her that Kingsley Palmer had torpedoed her favourite ghost story. It was that of Tom Dewfall who was said to have appeared in the street after he had died and warned a woman not to let her daughter sail on the Cunarder SS *Lusitania*. The girl was to have been among children from Blandford Grammar School who were being evacuated to America. German submarine U-20 put the *Lusitania* into 315 feet of water, with the loss of 1,198 lives, at 14.28 hours on 7 May 1916.

The hitch in the story line is that the *Lusitania* could not have been taking any British evacuees—she was sailing off Ireland, twelve miles from the Head of Kinsale, and into British waters at the time. The decisive fact was that the dead included 128 United States citizens—a fact that was to bring the sleeping tiger into the Great War.

It was a tragedy that made a massive impact on both sides of the Atlantic. Seventy years later, hanging on a barracks wall on Steep Holm island in the Bristol Channel, is a poster produced by the Parliamentary Recruitment Committee which shows Britannia rising from the water beside the sinking liner. "Avenge the sword of justice," it calls. In America it is remembered for one of the best exit lines in history. Broadway theatre owner Charles Frohman had eighteen minutes between the explosions and the sea to come out with this exercise in composure: "Why fear death? It is the most beautiful adventure in life." So what that it's derivative; J. M. Barrie didn't have to follow his original version by drowning.

Miss Knott could not accept that her story might be wrong when I read the debunking extract from the *Oral Folk-Tales of Wessex*. "I know it is right. I used to know the lady so well and she said it was the *Lusitania*. It has to be the *Lusitania*."

Kingsley Palmer suggested the *Athenia* sinking as an alternative. This was a disaster of similar proportions to an outward bound ship, but she went down in 1939 and Miss Knott was adamant that the age of her informant had to mean a First World War date. So drowns a good ghost story, but in its way it shows as much as most.

Whatever the absence of truth in this story, the *Lusitania* sinking scarred the memory of a generation. Independent of recorded history, the *Lusitania* and the *Titanic* would go on to everlasting life, via such fabulous tales of myriad miracles and horrors, and sail on as eternal voyagers in the epic sagas from the twentieth century.

SWANAGE

The fire blamed on a ghost

NEWSPAPER REPORTS of a fire at Newton Cottage in the High Street at Swanage began with references to "something of a ghostly nature" and pointed out that the building was reputedly haunted. Chief Fire Officer R. E. J. Paull had a more prosaic explanation for the blaze that took place on 11 December 1966: "It could have been caused by someone sleeping rough and leaving a cigarette end behind, or perhaps by children playing with matches."

The house had all the requirements for folkore to develop as it had been left for years in a time-warp, fully furnished with the beds made up, since the death of photographer William Cox was followed by that of his widow. They had left no family. The site had just been purchased, in 1966, by the Rotary Club of Swanage and Purbeck for its site value, and they intended clearing the house and securing planning permission for its replacement by four blocks of flats.

Meanwhile, stories of ghosts and down-and-outs were a useful device for Swanage parents to use to keep their more impressionable offspring away from potential danger. The fire, whatever agency might have caused it, was confined to a single room and stairway.

SWANAGE [hamlet of GODLINGSTON]

Face through the window

GODLINGSTON IS a house of grey stone walls and slates, one of the oldest inhabited buildings in Purbeck, set in National Trust land at the foot of Nine Barrow Down near the Ulwell gap [Ordnance Survey map reference SZ 014 802]. Said to have eight hundred years of history, the house presents a long, low elevation to its grounds and retreats behind small mullioned windows tightly held by the gaunt facade. Here Mrs. Jean Bowerman had been told of the ghost of a lady who was supposed to walk by the garden wall, "but seven years ago, I think, she decided to look in through a window when I was working late. I didn't see her, but had I been a dog, my hair would have stood on end as I felt her presence. Not appreciating the feeling, I fled."

Mrs. Bowerman gradually forgot her experience until a former occupant of Godlingston came to tea: during conversation, this lady said that her husband had seen the ghost through the same window. "Now, alas, the ghost seems to have taken a fancy to the upstairs landing and she's even more of a deterrent than the slugs to going down at night. Not that I'm afraid—let's just say that I prefer not to look behind me on the landing."

She recalled the occurrence for the Farmers Weekly of 29 September 1967.

TARRANT GUNVILLE

The steward who lives on as a vampire

WILLIAM DOGGETT was the steward of Eastbury at Tarrant Gunville when it was one of the greatest mansions in the land. It had been embellished regardless of expense, in the 1720s, by George Bubb Dodington who spent £140,000—compared with the contemporary £250,000 for Blenheim Palace—to complete what had been his uncle's ambition and vision. Dodington frequented the corridors of power, and was an absentee palace owner. He was created Baron Melcombe in 1761, the year before he died, and enjoyed a national reputation for corruption, as did his steward locally.

Because of his master's incessant absences Doggett took little trouble to cover his frauds. Then, according to the tale that was handed down in the Bugle Horn, the watering hole at the park gates, for generations to come, he had the unexpected news that Dodington was standing beside the Blandford road. He had just alighted from the London mail coach. With evidence of his fiddles all around, and only minutes in which to do anything, Doggett did the first decent thing of his life. He went into the library, closed the door, and shot himself.

In 1795 Lord Temple demolished all but a wing of Eastbury House and it is at the park gates [Ordnance Survey map reference ST 927 127] that Doggett is said to have a perpetual existence. He appears as a figure from another age, at midnight, wearing a wig and with knee-breeches tied with yellow silk ribbon. He is waiting for his coach and this, it turns out, has a headless coachman driving headless horses. They take Doggett back up the drive to the house. He enters and re-enacts his suicide.

In the Bugle Horn they believed that Doggett was un-dead, who unworthy of burial in consecrated ground would live on as a vampire to emerge from his tomb at night to drink the blood of sleeping villagers. Their story in justification of this is that when the parish church at Tarrant Gunville was demolished in the nineteenth century Doggett's corpse was found not to have decomposed and the legs were bound together with a ribbon of yellow silk.

A soldier's hand

DEER STEALING was for many years frequently and violently engaged in by the men from villages around Cranborne Chase, and in growing desperation the poachers banded together, groups of nocturnal raiders being ready to attack any keepers they encountered. Each side was heavily armed with guns, pistols, flails and quarter staffs: with tough straw hats as protection for their heads. One such serious affray occurred on the night of 16 December 1780 at Chettle Common and was between a party of seven deer hunters and five keepers. The leader of the poachers was a Trumpet Major of a regiment of dragoons then quartered at Blandford and whose name was also Blandford. This officer left the battle minus one of his hands which was severed from the arm by a keeper's hanger.

Severe wounds were received on both sides and one of the keepers eventually died of his injuries. Blandford and the gang were later captured and taken to Dorchester where they were sentenced to seven years transportation but, in consideration of their wounds, this verdict was commuted to imprisonment.

Blandford's hand was buried in Pimperne churchyard and is said to wander at night in search of its owner and haunts the ride known as Bussey Stool Walk. In superstitious times it was believed to be highly ill-advised for a body not to have been buried intact, as would have been the case when Blandford finally died—the hand should then have been reunited with the corpse.

William Chafin, in 1818, recalled the details of the affray in his *Anecdotes and History of Cranbourn Chase*:

"Blandford's arm was tightly bound with a list garter to prevent its bleeding and he was carried to the Lodge, where I saw him the following day, and his hand in the window. Peter Beckford, Esq. who was at that time Ranger of the Walk, came in the morning and brought Mr. Dansey, a very eminent surgeon, with him, who dressed the wound and administered proper remedies to the poor patient. Two young Officers came also in the course of the day to see him. As soon as he was well enough to be removed he was committed, with his companions, to Dorchester gaol. The hand was buried in Pimperne churchyard and, as reported, with the honours of war.

"The soldier was not dismissed from His Majesty's service, but suffered to retire upon half-pay, or pension; and set up a shop in London, which he denoted a Game factor's, and dispersed handbills at all the public passages, in order to get customers, one of which he himself put into my hand in the archway leading into Lincoln's Inn Square."

Much of the old woodland at Bussey Stool Walk has since been felled. A road runs up a dry chalk coombe from Tarrant Gunville village to Bussey Stool. Where the road turns sharply left into a farmyard, a track continues straight ahead to Bloody Shard Gate [Ordnance Survey map reference ST 933 148] at the meeting place of several paths. Its name preserves the memory of these events. The field between the gate and Bussey Stool Farm is called Bloody Field and the woodland that used to stretch away to the north of the gate, far more than it does today, was known as Bloodway Coppice.

THORNCOMBE
[hamlet of FORDE]

Forde Abbey:
its dead
continue their
ownership dispute.

Coffins afloat

DEVON'S FAMOUS Forde Abbey, which now lies inside the bounds of Dorset [Ordnance Survey map reference ST 359 053], inevitably has its ghost stories. It was a Cistercian monastery before the year 1200, being one of the religious houses founded during the general religious revival of the twelfth century and it was still one of the largest in Devon (that is, one of the few left in the county with more than a dozen monks) when, on 8 March 1539, its monastic life ended. It was one of the last monasteries in Devon to be suppressed by the Dissolution.

Following that, and the damage it then suffered at the hands of the henchmen of Henry VIII, it remained in something of a decay until its glories were restored by a secular owner, Sir Edmond Prideaux. The Prideaux family, flourishing over the second part of the sixteenth century and for much of the following century, were typical of many such English country families of around that time, whose younger sons went into politics or the professions. In the case of the Prideaux family it was the law. Being able to put together some sizeable sums of money, they began their own families and estates, often by purchase. Hence the Prideaux ownership of Forde. The last Prideaux provides one of Forde's ghost stories.

Under its chapel are two vaults. The second is higher than the first because the first was chronically waterlogged, due, probably, to seepage from the nearby River Axe into its too-low level. In the first vault the coffins had to be raised from the ground. In the second, which was higher and consequently drier, they were placed on the ground.

Stories began to circulate of voices being heard by persons working in the chapel. Some took to their heels, declaring that the voices were coming up from the vaults beneath; men's voices, two men quarrelling violently, and strange thudding kinds of noises-off into the bargain. Screwing up their courage, some of the bolder spirits listened hard, ultimately coming to the conclusion that both vaults were completely flooded with the coffins floating about, and that every time Edmond Prideaux's coffin (he was the last Forde Prideaux) collided head-on with that of Francis Gwyn (Forde passing to the Gwyn family due to lack of direct Prideaux succession) the occupants began a noisy dispute. But precisely what they said to each other as they collided nobody seemed to know. The actual bumping into each other, and presumably the other family coffins down there colliding too, with the walls as well as with each other, were causing the mysterious noises. All very alarming indeed, and a very plausible story.

Later the mundane trouble of excessive damp at Forde caused an exploration of the two vaults themselves. This put paid to the more sensational features of the story, for the vaults were not—and had not been—completely awash, and in any case, even if they had been, the coffins would have been unlikely to have floated about, being made of lead and weighing six hundredweight apiece. Whether or not quarrelling voices and noises were heard, and what may have been their origin, remains unanswered. Perhaps some trick of acoustics should not be overlooked as a possible explanation.

Forde's other ghost stories derive from its monks, the most cogent concerning Thomas Chard, its last Abbot.   A sincere, good and courageous man, by all reports, he tried his utmost to stem the tide of monastic suppression engulfing the religious houses of the West.   Although he did, in fact, manage to save many of the glories of Forde from despoliation and total destruction, he suffered the sorrow and chagrin of witnessing the desecration of much that he, himself, had created in those latter years.   For, so it is presumed, he had deemed that the best defence from the troubles inevitably looming as Henry's dispute with Rome escalated, was a well-disciplined and well-maintained religious house.   Although it would seem he failed, he probably did, by his foresight, save Forde from the fate of Newenham Abbey where, today, not a trace remains.

His venue is said to be the refectory, some accounts having him seated at the refectory table.   In those last days of the monasteries the life of its inmates was fairly comfortable both as to its accommodation and its provender, for the religious houses were in being long enough for them to have accumulated considerable land.   However, his appearances are reputedly very infrequent, so nobody need visit Forde with the idea of meeting him.

This story, which I wrote with Mary Collier for our *Ghosts of Dorset, Devon and Somerset*, was questioned in Pulman's Weekly News of 7 March 1978 by the owner of Forde Abbey.   Mrs. Mark Roper could not accept the acoustic explanation and said that the vaults had been awash and were filled with earth because of the eerie noises.   The reporter, Chris Carson, tended to agree: "Today, water had again flooded into the vaults which lay concealed beneath a wooden door in the floor of the chapel.   When we visited the site water was almost waist deep but the coffins seemed well secured.   Even so, Mrs. Roper said, ghosts or not, she would not care to go down there."

A ghost story that might have been came from the banks of the River Axe near Forde at the end of the 1970s.   There were puzzling reports of a large, furry aquatic creature.   Its appearance coincided, however, with scores of poplars and willow trees being felled by a terminal knawing on their river-facing sides.   The culprit turned out to be a beaver—an escapee from Cricket St Thomas Wild Life Park.

TYNEHAM [hamlet of WORBARROW]

A smuggler's death

THE LEGEND of the smuggler is set at Worbarrow Bay, where the hog's back of the hilly spine of Purbeck plunges 550 feet to the sea, its great expanse of chalk contrasting with the multi-coloured sands of the lower cliffs at Worbarrow itself. At the far end of the long, lonely bay, sometime in the eighteenth century, a solitary smuggler was startled by a group of revenue men.   He was unfamiliar with this part of the coast and ran along the beach, till he found himself facing a sheer wall of unclimbable rock at Cow Corner [Ordnance Survey map reference SY 860 804].

The custom men closed in on their trapped prey who turned to the sea, where, in dark, still water, he was murdered by stoning.   His gasping screams, the splashing caused by the convulsions of his body, and then the silence of the night, can be heard at the waning of the moon. This tale of the brutal death of a defenceless smuggler, at a place as remote as any in Dorset, conflicts with the usual romantic flavour which has come lately to be associated with smuggling.

UPLYME [hamlet of ROCOMBE]

Masked coachman

ALTHOUGH GHOSTLY coach stories are legion in Somerset they are not so common in either Devon or Dorset. But from the border parish of Uplyme, north of Lyme Regis, comes one of the most intriguing, more particularly so because the beholder was a child, who, noting its details in the way a child will of any object that may specially interest him, did so without realising he was looking at something supernatural.

A naturally and indubitably truthful boy, he has seen no such other phenomenon before or since, and, apart from his natural veracity, as his adults point out, he could hardly have made up the details of persons and coach, and neither would he—strongest evidence of all—have left the other children and run home crying because "he'd seen a coach which disappeared and nobody was going to believe him!"

What was worrying him was not what he'd just seen, but the resultant possible aspersions on his truthfulness, his devil-and-deep-sea being that either he must keep the odd experience to himself or be suspected of lying. But bit by bit the story came out.

At the time he was nine; in 1973 he was twelve, and still told the story quite freely. The place was the Old Coaching Road at a point called locally "up by the white gate." It is on the road that drops down to Rocombe [Ordnance Survey map reference SY 325 951] from Whitty Hill, on one of the back ways from Uplyme to Raymond's Hill. The boy was accompanied by his sister, their cousin and their donkey, and none of the others saw the coach except himself, because he, having borrowed a bigger cousin's bicycle, had ridden on ahead of the main party by quite a way. At that point the others could not have seen the coach because of the formation of the road.

Here is his story, told three years after the event: "I saw a big coach, a stage coach, like you see in pictures of coaches. The top part was red and the lower part had black and gold trimmings. It had four horses, three were black and one was white, and the coachman wore a mask over his face, not all over it, but over the top part like the 'eye-masks' you see in pictures, and he had a big red feather over his hat. There were two men riding outside at the back. The coach drew out of the white gate, as if it was going towards Lyme, and it was coming towards me, too. I was looking straight at it. Then I looked away for some reason—I can't remember why—just for a minute—and when I looked that way again the coach had vanished. There wasn't a sign of it. It made no sound and I thought the men had cruel sort of faces and I wondered if they'd got a prisoner inside."

Apparently the outlines of the coach were not quite so clear as those of an ordinary vehicle at such a place and distance would have been, yet there was

nothing that immediately struck him as odd, that is, apart from meeting a convey-
ance of that type, until he realised that it had vanished.

[This piece was written by Mary Collier and myself for *Ghosts of Dorset, Devon
and Somerset*, 1974.]

UPLYME [hamlet of YAWL]

Monmouth on a white horse

THE ROAD from Uplyme to Yawl, north-west of Lyme Regis, is believed to be
haunted by the ghost of the Duke of Monmouth in person. This section of road
is only about half-a-mile long and the main section is now the A3070 [Ordnance
Survey map reference SY 319 940]. The Duke would have ridden up this lane as
he moved out of Lyme at the start of his 1685 rebellion.

"He rides from Yawl to Uplyme on his white horse, always at night and
sometimes around midnight," it is said. The figure is emphatically declared to be
Monmouth himself and he is said to be in possession of his head. Here he is not
apparently in flight, but trots at normal speed. The ghost has been heard more
recently than it has been sighted.

At one of the houses in the valley, beside the road, the family were disturbed
one night by the sound of trotting. The daughter of the house thought that the
ponies had escaped from the stable. A keen rider, she hastily dressed and went
out with other members of the family to round them up. But although they
could hear trotting clearly enough, not a horse nor a pony was to be seen
anywhere, and their own ponies were peacefully in the stable. The sound could
not be accounted for by any break-loose from neighbouring houses or farms
because no-one else kept horses or ponies.

[This piece was written by Mary Collier and myself for *Ghosts of Dorset, Devon
and Somerset*, 1974.]

WEST LULWORTH

**Durdle Door –
a dance macabre.**

Sea-maidens at Durdle Door

AFTER THE magnificent Weld family residence at Lulworth Castle, in its own
parkland at East Lulworth, was gutted by fire in 1929 there was a local story that
the maidservants had disappeared. Certainly the maids were never seen again
but the rational explanation was that they had taken the train home after their
workplace and possessions had been destroyed.

The story grew, however, that all twelve of them had gone for a walk that day
along the cliff path to Durdle Door and been washed into the sea from the
forty-foot high arch of rock.

Jill Curnock Dick sent me the legend in 1968, with an explanation that she had
heard it from a former naval commander, living in retirement at Poole, who was

in his cabin when a "wild crescendo of screams" tore the night air, back in the 1930s. He was at anchor off Lulworth. "I leapt up the companion ladder," he said, "my throat scalding with fear. Desperately I sought to penetrate the wall of darkness to the north, frantically searching to divide water from shore as the shrieking inferno raged about me.

"Then the screaming stopped, as abruptly as if the dark waters had quenched it for ever, and a small evanescent form rose on what I could just distinguish as the foreshore, not two hundred yards from my boat. It was the figure of a child.

"As it developed substance I saw it was a young girl.

"Her white expressionless face jerked awkwardly in a macabre dance. Soon she was joined by another figure, and then another, and another. At once the foreshore was peopled with ten or a dozen girlish wraiths prancing and leaping in a mournful travesty of a childhood game.

"They were a ghastly spectacle, and utterly joyless.

"Suddenly, the figures were still, as if restrained by a noiseless command, grew faint and were gone. I forced my eyes to stare harder. But the curved foreshore was empty."

WEYMOUTH

Heavy footsteps in the Boot Inn

WHEN LICENSEE John Ratcliffe and his wife Elsie took over the Boot Inn at Weymouth in 1973 they were warned by their predecessor that the pub was haunted. The former landlord is said to have caught the intruder singing sea shanties one night. The Boot Inn was built about 1650 and stands in High West Street, opposite the Old Town Hall, behind North Quay on the southern side of the Backwater.

The new tenants had only been at the inn a week when on two nights they heard the ghost clumping around the bars. Mr. Ratcliffe went downstairs to investigate and saw nothing: "But the bang of his boots on the floorboards continued and they went right through me."

His wife stayed upstairs: "I was too frightened to go down. John went both times. It's really creepy." Mr. and Mrs. Ratcliffe were reported in the Dorset Evening Echo of 23 November 1973, saying they would prefer to see something rather than have to endure the un-nerving tread of invisible feet: "If our friend continues his nightly walks, we have only one request. We hope he will let us get a visual glimpse of him sometime."

WHITCHURCH CANONICORUM

Meeting a Saint

IN THE late 1930s, Jack Bowditch drove from the Marshwood Vale to the railway station at Axminster to pick up a lady who was visiting his employer. She said she would have some time to spare and asked if there were any local places of interest.   Mr. Bowditch suggested Forde Abbey and the parish church at Whitchurch Canonicorum, which has been called "the Cathedral of the Vale".

It shares the distinction, with Westminster Abbey, of being otherwise the only church in the land to house the shrine and relics of its patron saint, St. Wite.   Her legends are discussed at the end of this book, but for now we shall hear the experiences of the lady, who happened to mention to Mr. Bowditch that she was psychic.

Sylvia Creed gives the punch-line to what she asserts is a true story in her account of *Dorset's Western Vale*, 1987: "The next morning this lady walked to Whitchurch and was gone for over three hours.   When she returned to the house at Morcombelake her face was white as a sheet and she went straight to her room.   When she emerged sometime later she told of how whilst in the church she saw a little old lady in white sitting in a pew crying.   She went over to the lady and asked whether she could help her.   The woman in white sadly shook her head and then vanished from sight.   The visitor believed that the apparition was that of St. Wite."

WHITCHURCH CANONICORUM

Road signs and exorcism

A PHANTOM coach that was reputed to make midnight appearances on the pre-bypass course of the A35 to the east of Charmouth, up the hill at Newlands in the south-west corner of the parish of Whitchurch Canonicorum, took the blame for a spate of road accidents.   Rational minds reasoned that some of the crashes at least were caused by the bumps in the road, which was slowly sliding northwards down the hill towards the River Char.

Both opinions led to positive actions in the 1960s.   Council roadmen erected "Liable to subsidence" signs on the hill [Ordnance Survey map reference SY 373 936] and to counteract the supernatural there was the intervention of bell, book and candle.   Rev. Dr. Donald Omand, the vicar of Chideock, carried out a ceremony of exorcism.

WHITCHURCH CANONICORUM

Ghostly white cow

GHOSTLY COWS are rare but Whitchurch Canonicorum, on the edge of the Marshwood Vale, has produced one since the last war and it was seen by two men.   It was a clear, dark evening and they were crossing a field, taking a short cut to a friend's farm.   One of them told us:

"We noticed a white cow in the field.   We didn't take any particular notice of it beyond that one doesn't very often see all-white cows.   Some farmers are very superstitious about them and make out they are unlucky.   So when we got to the farmhouse we said to him that we didn't know he'd got a white cow. 'But I haven't,' he said. 'I've never had one. But I'll have a look around in the morning. She must belong to someone near and have strayed here but I can't think of anyone who has one.'''

The two young farmers thought no more of the incident until they saw their friend again some weeks later. "You remember that white cow you told me about," he said. "Well, the nearest white cow to me is twenty miles away and she certainly wasn't straying that evening. I made sure about that. You two saw a ghost!''

WIMBORNE

Reverend Percy Newall

KING'S HOUSE, West Borough, Wimborne, is haunted by a ghost who rises at six o'clock each morning and is heard opening a heavy, but now blocked, doorway in the wall of an upstairs room. This old building adjoins Dickens House and an elderly lady, who stayed there during the war, often spoke of seeing a clergyman appearing through the wall, opposite the blocked doorway in the next house. Dressed in black with a Bible under his arm, the figure is reputed to be the Rev. Percy Newall who owned King's House, which was then called Garden House, between 1843 and 1875.

WIMBORNE ST. GILES

The horseman vanished

THE ONLY authenticated sighting in Dorset of the ghost of a prehistoric man was that encountered by an archaeologist, Dr. R. C. C. Clay of Fovant, Wiltshire, whilst driving along the B3081 road between Cranborne and Handley Cross. The incident occurred during the winter of 1927 when Dr. Clay was excavating an urnfield at Pokesdown. One night he was returning home along that stretch of road, when about 150 yards past Squirrel's Corner he saw a horseman on the downs to the north-east, travelling in his direction.

Dr. Clay's account of his experiences is given in *Dorset Barrows* by Leslie Grinsell, F.S.A., an authoritative study of the county's burial mounds by an eminent archaeologist, which has become the standard work of its type. Mr. Grinsell was given this account of the horseman:

"Thinking he was from the training stables at Nine Yews, I took very little notice of him at first. Suddenly he turned his horse's head and galloped as if to reach the road ahead, before my car arrived there. I was so interested that I changed gear to slow my car's speed in order that we should meet, and I should be able to find out why he had taken this sudden action. Before I had drawn level with him, he turned his horse again to the north, and galloped along parallel to me about 50 yards from the road. I could now see that he was no ordinary horseman, for he had bare legs, and wore a long, loose coat. The horse had a long mane and tail, but I could see no bridle or stirrups. The rider's face was turned towards me, but I could not see his features. He seemed to be threatening me with some implement which he waved in his right hand above his head. I tried hard to identify the weapon, for I suddenly realised that he was a prehistoric man; but I failed. It seemed to be on a two-foot shaft. After travelling parallel to my car for about 100 yards, the rider and horse suddenly vanished. I noted the spot, and the next day found at the spot a low round barrow."

This barrow is numbered "Wimborne St. Giles 35" in Mr. Grinsell's list of about two thousand ancient burial mounds in Dorset. It lies on the wide verge beside the B3081 at Bottlebush Down, 1,200 yards south-east of Handley Cross [Ordnance Survey map reference SU 020 159]. On the north side of the road, it is grass covered with a diameter of fifteen paces and height of four feet. When approaching from Handley, you cross the five feet high original carriageway of the Roman road Ackling Dyke and then the bank of an earthwork known as the Dorset Cursus, before reaching the barrow, which lies on your left. Cranborne Chase around this part is a landscape as scarred with prehistoric earthworks as any in Britain—despite the passing of 3,500 years the scenery from this point, for as far as you can see, retains more marks of the Bronze Age than it has gained from any period since. If ghosts have survived from such a lost age, then here they can be expected to appear.

Mr. Grinsell's note concludes: "A few years ago, the late Alexander Keiller reported to Dr. Clay that two girls, returning from Cranborne to Handley from a dance, had complained to the policeman at Handley that they had been followed and frightened by a man on horseback. Within the last thirty years there have been other reports, from shepherds and others, of apparitions having been seen in the vicinity of Bottlebush Down."

WIMBORNE ST. GILES

The white lady of Bone Acre Copse

THE B3078 road from Wimborne to Cranborne passes through some ancient wood-land at the edge of St. Giles's Park. The road separates the park's Drive Plan-tation from the denser expanse of Bone Acre Copse [Ordnance Survey map reference SU 043 107] as you approach the Verwood turning nearly two miles from Cranborne. This copse is said to be haunted by a hooded lady, dressed in white, who sometimes ventures on to the highway but crashes back into the undergrowth as soon as she is spotted.

Sound is strongly associated with this spectre. In pre-motor car days she was heard rushing through the trees. Moments later there was said to be a much louder roar as a wagon and horses careered between the trees. The sound then continued for a matter of minutes but the phantom coach was never sighted. The wood is strongly associated with violent events—at least one wayside murder being dimly recalled—and tree-fellers have disturbed skeletons. It seems to contain a prehistoric or Roman cemetery which made sufficient impres-sion on those who worked there to provide its name, Bone Acre Copse.

WINTERBORNE STICKLAND/DEWLISH

Mr. Skinner is none too happy

KINGSLEY PALMER noted in his *Oral Folk-Tales of Wessex* [1973] that as ghosts are essentially pagan objects one does not expect them in Christian churches. Not that I agree with him; a resurrection was at the basis of this religion's faith, and in theory still should be. Dorset churches have provided ecclesiastical ghosts for this present book—I am thinking of those at Dorchester and Silton—and they are abundant around abbeys.

The church ghost that Palmer found was not of a cleric but a notable land-owner. Thomas Skinner of Dewlish, in the chalk downlands between Dorchester and Blandford, was interred in the parish church at Winterborne Stickland. This village is six miles north-east of Dewlish; and it seems he is none too happy there. Skinner died at the age of sixty-eight on 5 October 1756 and was buried in the family vault beneath the chancel aisle. His widow, Barbara, is also there, having died on 13 December 1769, aged seventy. She left £200 for bread to feed the parish poor.

Mr. Skinner has been given the credit for knocking books off the altar. When they were picked up there was said to have been a pool of blood on the floor.

Palmer's informant provides a sighting: "He was seen one night during a power cut by the choir and congregation at Evensong. He appeared to walk across from the Skinner Chapel to the altar and look at the congregation. Perhaps he was used to having his rest disturbed at the same time on Sunday, and wondered what the sudden darkness was for. The previous rector, Canon Low, is reputed to have seen him many times in the church, and was firmly convinced there was a ghost."

Vandals entered the Skinner chapel in 1969 and tried to prise Skinner's black marble memorial slab from its plinth—not that he is under there—which pro-voked a week of sightings.

Dewlish, incidentally, is spelt "Develish" on the Skinner inscription. The village takes its name from the Devil's Brook.

WINTERBOURNE ABBAS

The unpredictable water spirit

THE DORSET "winterbornes" have been obvious candidates for a belief in water spirits since pre-Celtic times, for in a year of average weather they dry out in the summer and then run again after the autumn rains. The turning on of the tap was regarded as an act of the gods and indeed those of us who regularly drive by sections of such streams notice they are grass-covered one day and water-filled the next.

"No man will ever see a winter-borne break," was the superstition at Winterbourne Abbas and in verification of this they quote the time, in about the 1860s, that a stream-watch was mounted with villagers operating a rota day and night. The watcher waited above the village by the ancient Nine Stones which as an unexplained prehistoric survival added a touch of additional mystique [Ordnance Survey map reference SY 611 904].

The watch ended one evening when the South Winterborne Stream broke and spilt on down towards Winterbourne Steepleton, Martinstown, Winterbourne Monkton, Winterborne Herringston, Winterborne Came and the River Frome at West Stafford. Not that the watchman saw anything. He had walked up to the lodge to re-light his pipe.

"Baint bin gwone dree minuts and her had broke," he reported back to the village.

Woolbridge Manor [left] **and the mediaeval bridge** [right]
where a bus driver stopped for the spectral Turberville coach.

WOOL/BERE REGIS

The Turberville coach

WOOLBRIDGE MANOR, a Jacobean house beside the River Frome at Wool, was a seat of the Turbervilles, an old Dorset family whose headquarters were at Bere Regis, five miles to the north. A spectral coach-and-four is said to drive out from Woolbridge in the evening gloom, but can only be seen by those with Turberville blood in their veins. Thomas Hardy used the legend, with some embellishment, in *Tess of the D'Urbervilles*, the most depressing of his books. The four-in-hand goes between the manor at Woolbridge [Ordnance Survey map reference SY 844 873] and the site of the destroyed manor house at Bere Regis where, incidentally, the memorials to the Turberville family can be visited in the parish church [map reference SY 847 947].

The best modern account I have heard of the appearance of the coach came from a Durweston lady, Mrs. Mary E. Bradley, who was delivering a lecture on the historic houses of Dorset in the 1960s. Someone in the hall looked up at the mention of Woolbridge, and asked their speaker "Do you know the story of the driver who stopped the bus from Lulworth to Wareham on the bridge? It was in all the local papers; he stopped the bus and the passengers asked why, to which he replied, 'I baint gwoing to move ontil this thare coach be gwone dru they thare doors'."

This story was later related by the lecturer at an outdoor Women's Institute meeting near Woodsford Castle where, over a cup of tea, an elderly member said she knew the man well: "It's quite true, me dear, he always swore he saw something." To be in complete accord with the legend, the driver should have been a descendant of the Turberville line, and by some accounts the sight of the phantom coach is said to forebode disaster.

Vampire at the gates – Eastbury's steward
is undead in the leafy valley opposite
the Bugle Horn inn at Tarrant Gunville.
Doggett's story is on page 71.

Eater of babies – folklore surrounds
the Cerne Giant and stretches back
to the human sacrifices of the
Druidic Celts. The story of 'His Mightiness' is on page 101.

Thou shalt not suffer a witch to live.

— HOLY BIBLE [EXODUS xxii, 18]

WITCHCRAFT

This savage horned-mask was stolen from the Cave family of Holt Farm, Melbury Osmond, in 1897. It was an object made for active ceremonial as the jaw was hinged and there were memories of it being paraded in chains with 'lucifer matches pushed alight into the head'. Villagers called it the 'Ooser' (pronounced 'osser') which is probably a dialect survival of the Old English word 'wuduwasa' (satyr) as the initial 'w' tended to be dropped from Dorset speech. Oser is also the seventeenth century Italian word for the devil.

Archaeologist Tom Lethbridge had no doubt that the Ooser was a relic of mediaeval witchcraft and cited references from trials where the devil was said to be personified by 'a kind of stud-bull in relation to the women of his particular coven or group of covens'. He used an artificial phallus and penetrated them from behind with a sperm substitute. The devil's 'milk' was always cold. The devil's penis was said to be larger and more reliable than that of any man, and there is no doubt that sexual gratification played a key part in witchcraft's continuing appeal.

Lethbridge considered that this may have accounted for the theft of the Ooser from the 'tallet' (hayloft) at Holt Farm: 'One feels that it may have returned to some hidden coven in the area.'

And they think we're burning witches when we're only burning weeds.

— G. K. CHESTERTON [LEPANTO]

Bewitched fishing boats

HOLY STONES, or witch-stones as they are called, are those beach pebbles with a
natural hole in the centre.   They are also known as hag-stones and were often
tied to a door-key and carried around as a precaution against witches and evil
spirits.   Others would tie them to the cast-iron bedhead.   Again, the combination
of a holy stone and iron was a powerful preventive measure.

In Dorset, in the late 1830s and 40s, it was not uncommon to see such stones
dangling from the large open rowing boats at Weymouth.   They would hang
from nails or staples close beneath the gunwale, the upper edge of timber running
round the boat's side.   In this way the stones could be used in conjunction with
iron.

Sometimes, at Abbotsbury, a boat would fail to catch any fish even though
there might be great shoals all around and the other boats in the party would be
hauling full nets on to the Chesil Bank.   The unlucky boat would be considered
bewitched.   And the only way this spell could be broken was to attach a mackerel, liberally stuck with pins, to the rudder.

Abbotsbury's annual pagan survival was Garland Day on 13 May—preserving
the May Day of the pre-1722 calendar—when flower-covered structures were
carried on poles around the village and then on to the beach where, in shades of
the fertility cult, games and festivities took place.   All the village took part and
the garlands were finally placed in the fishing boats and taken out to sea where
they were cast overboard to drift on the waves.

Inland, other methods of witch-prevention were used.   Ralph Wightman gave
a traditional Dorset method of avoiding being overlooked by the evil eye when he
took part in a "Country Questions" broadcast on 24 May, 1964.   Tie a knot of
Mountain Ash into a cross, he said, and then thread this into the hairs of a cow's
tail.

[This piece was part of the additional material written by me for Olive Knott's
Witches of Dorset, 1974.]

The Head who was 'overlooked'

WHEN LOIS WALKER was appointed by the local squire, Sir Ernest Debenham, to the
headship of Affpuddle village school, she was aware that things are done differently in the country.   The day after arrival in 1921 she was awoken by a group
of men who proceeded to push a holly tree into a house for the purpose of
sweeping the chimney.   In the fields it was a customary sight in early summer to
see baby birds that had been taken from their nests and impaled on the barbed
wire of the fences.   "Superstitious beliefs still linger," she wrote in her reminiscences of *A School among the Puddles*:

"I was warned to be very careful with the school cleaner because she could 'overlook me'. I was amused at the time, but I found the school locked one morning and the key missing from the cleaner's porch. I had to send for the blacksmith to remove the lock.

"A week later the coal-house key was lost; later the key from a class-room door. I began to think there was something in the 'overlooking' warning and asked a School Manager if another cleaner could be appointed, but he refused to help; possibly he might think the 'overlooking' would be transferred to him. However, when the key to the County Library box vanished, I appealed to the Director of Education and he wrote and asked the Managers to appoint another cleaner. Thus the curse was lifted—a few years later a hole was dug for a foot-scraper by the back door and there were the missing keys."

BLANDFORD

The case of the mummified cat

THE DISCOVERY in May 1963 of the mummified body of a cat sealed in the wall of a cottage being demolished at Blandford started speculation that the animal might have been a witch's familiar or have been involved in some ritual sacrifice. It was found standing on a ledge about six feet from the floor, sandwiched between a lath-and-plaster partition and a brick wall. Only a few inches away was a volume of prose and poetry published in 1851.

This was entitled *The Speaker*, with the explanation that it contained "miscellaneous pieces selected from the best English writers, with a view to facilitating the improvement of youth in reading and speaking." Inside the cover was an inscription: "John Chaffey, from his sincere friend and well-wisher, James Hunt, 3 Victoria Terrace, Swanage, Oct. 12/63."

Said Mr. Jack Raymond of Milton Abbas, who demolished the building: "The wall was completely plastered up, and there was no sign of any opening, so I don't see how the cat could have got in there by accident. The book was bound in black, and someone who saw it suggested that somebody, unable to read or write, might have placed it beside the body of the cat thinking it was a Bible."

The cottage was number six, Whitecliff Mill Street, and now lies under part of Fiander's garage. Mrs. Grace James, wife of the newsagent at the Plocks, told a reporter the building had been the home of her family shop there.

The point that cats do sometimes come to a natural end inside cavity walls, through their own curiosity, was made in a letter to a local newspaper a couple of weeks later. Mr. R. G. Tapper wrote that when No. 51 Durweston was being repaired by estate workmen in 1903 they found the mummified body of a ginger cat: "It was in a good state of preservation, completely flat. Claws and the whiskers were in perfect condition. I showed the body to the late William Green, who lived there previously, and he identified it as a cat he had lost many

[This piece was part of the additional material written by me for Olive Knott's *Witches of Dorset*, 1974.]

years before.   He also remembered that at the time the cat was missing, the wall was being repaired, and the cavity was left open overnight.   The workmen finished bricking up the hole the next morning, unaware that the cat was inside."

GILLINGHAM

Unemployed because he was 'overlooked'

IN THE late nineteenth century a Gillingham man of about fifty applied for poor relief to the guardians of the Shaftesbury Union Workhouse on the grounds that he was unable to work.   A doctor had seen him and confirmed his inability to labour but was unable to specify a medical cause.   The man himself claimed he was 'overlooked'—by his sister in law.

The man's wife had visited a "wise woman" at Stalbridge and this brought relief for a few days but then the spell returned and was even more potent.   He declined medicines saying they would be useless.

The outcome of the case is not recorded.

HILTON [hamlet of ANSTY]

An old crone and a cartwheel

FAR FROM any towns, in the centre of the Dorset Downs, Hall and Woodhouse had a brewery in the remote hamlet of Ansty where a number of tracks converge from distant parts of the chalkland heights and from the Blackmore Vale below. Theirs was the one industry in the district and the brewery used to employ most of the local labour force which came from scattered farms and cottages.   These people seldom had a break from country living and it was even rare to make the journey to a market town.   So for this lonely upland community the firm's annual outing was considered the event of the year.

On one such occasion early in the twentieth century a party set out for Weymouth packed close together on the hard benches of horse-drawn wagons.   After a twenty mile journey they arrived at Weymouth and all went well.   The summer weather permitted bathing, paddling and all the delights of the side-shows along the front, but as the long day drew to its close, clouds began to gather and by the time the party assembled for the return journey the rain fell in torrents.   There was a rush for the one wagon which was covered and a young woman in the company who had travelled down in one of the other conveyances took a seat in the covered wagon.

An old crone, whose seat she had taken, looked into the wagon and demanded her place.   The girl, however, refused to give it up.

The old woman, then, shaking her fist at the girl, called out, "You mark my words, you won't get home tonight."

With that she withdrew and found a seat in one of the uncovered vehicles.

The wagon started off in the pouring rain. Those without cover reached home safely, despite the discomfort of rain trickling down the necks of the occupants who huddled beneath old sacks or coats or anything which could be found.

But, before the covered wagon had travelled very far a wheel came off and the unfortunate occupants, delayed by the search for someone to assist them, did not reach home till morning.

[This piece was among material adapted by me for Olive Knott's *Witches of Dorset*, 1974.]

LEIGH

Mizmaze and the Witches of Fake-lore

WILLIAM BARNES mixed up two Leigh place-names in Joseph Glanvill's *Sadducismus Triumphatus* of 1681 and transposed the "Witches Corner" of Leigh Common at Bayford, near Wincanton, with the parish of Leigh, near Sherborne which has Dorset's only surviving mediaeval maze [on Leigh Hill, above Maze [or Back] Drove, at grid reference ST 620 182]. In her *Witches of Wessex*, Olive Knott compounded the muddle by moving the spot a further thirty miles to a third Leigh Common on the east side of Wimborne.

There is no doubt about the whereabouts of the Leigh Common mentioned in the 1664 trial of Elizabeth Style and Alice Duke of Wincanton who were convicted of witchcraft. The depositions detailing the evidence were all testified by inhabitants of Bayford—Walter Thicke, Elizabeth Foarwood and Nicholas Lambert—and Leigh Common is at the east end of the hamlet, beside the A303 [grid reference ST 745 297].

What the hexagonal earthwork at Dorset's Leigh did have, until the custom fell out of use before 1800, was a gathering of "the young men of the village to scour out the trenches and pare the banks once in six or seven years, and the day appropriated for the purpose was passed in rustic merriment and festivity". Only a raised central platform shows on the surface inside the seventy-five feet wide earthwork under normal conditions but its layout will have survived under the turf and sometimes the layout of the paths is visible as puddles after heavy rain.

Labyrinthine maze designs and the festivities of treading these cherished spots are lost in the mists of time and had their origins in the Mediterranean cultures some four thousand years ago. They have spread to peoples all over the world. The Leigh example, with concentric circles, is of the twelve-ring design which appeared at Chartres and other European cathedrals in the 1200s. Jeremy Harte has surveyed their Dorset associations in issue 113 of the Dorset County Magazine.

Mazes are among the most obscure earthworks in the field of British archaeology, having parallels in the Cretan and Egyptian labyrinths, and probably mark the sites of prehistoric dancing grounds. They are inextricably bound up with the rituals of life, death and fertility in the ages when the Celtic paganism of the old religion held sway in these islands. Like Christmas and the other fixed festivals of Christianity, mazes were a symbol of the past so strong that adoption instead of suppression was the method by which their power could be transferred and assimilated into the thought processes of Christ's millennium.   Mazes were set in the floors of cathedrals in Italy and France.

In England, a handful of what are probably genuine prehistoric mazes have survived in a Celtic setting.   On the open downland of Cranborne Chase, at Breamore Down near Whitsbury, a maze with shallow ditches separated by grassy banks lies on a ridge surrounded by Iron Age field systems.   Likewise, the disappeared maze on the Pimperne side of Blandford is in an area marked by the lines and depressions of intensive prehistoric occupation and farming. Another lies inside the Iron Age fort of St. Catherine's Hill at Winchester.

The immediate environs of Dorchester contain placenames which give clues to those who wish to trace its distant past.   As in Ireland, where the so-called "pleasant hills" have been defined as "ceremonial hills," the Mount Pleasant near Thomas Hardy's Max Gate home has been confirmed by excavation as a Bronze Age sacred circle.   On the chalk slopes on the other side of the Frome, is a small collection of farm buildings and cottages beside the main road to Puddletown.   Its name is Troy Town.

Mazes are often known at "Troytowns" and Virgil described the "game of Troy" played as in Crete where "the labyrinth of old between blind walls its secret hid from view."   So-called "Troy games" were performed by the young men of the royal household of Edward II in their military ride and tournament held on every Sunday in Lent.

Witches and fairies, too, are remembered in conjunction with mazes—"the yellow skirted fays, fly after the night steeds, leaving their moon-loved maze."

[Part of this piece is from additional material written by me for Olive Knott's *Witches of Dorset*, 1974.]

LYME REGIS

The perils of smoking

A SEVENTEENTH CENTURY case of witchcraft in Dorset occurred at Lyme Regis where, on 1 June 1687, Deanes Gimmerton, a local housewife, was tried on several charges of 'bewitching' her young neighbours.

The case was brought by Richard Scorch, whose eighteen-year-old son Nathaniel had become ill the previous April after smoking tobacco from a pipe which Deanes Gimmerton had prepared, and offered him.   At first he suffered only weakness and general debilitation.   On 23 May, he was taken with a violent fit lasting two hours—six people were needed to hold him down in his bed.   The fits continued and grew stronger.

Whenever he was taken with one of his fits, Nathaniel saw the apparition of Deanes Gimmerton.   After several of these violent sessions, several pins and one iron nail were discovered in various parts of his body.   Deanes always appeared to him at the same spot in the room; and when his family struck at the spot he indicated, his pain only increased, so that he begged them not to do anything. He remained weak and "in a pining and languishing condition."

Another witness was Mary Tillman, whose daughter Elizabeth was taken ill in the same way in 1682, when she too was eighteen. She had the same fits and also saw the apparition of Deanes Gimmerton. Brass pins were found on her body, and when her family tried to destroy them, Elizabeth's pain increased. In one of her fits, she was unable to move over from the stool where she was sitting, to her bed, and she said that Deanes Gimmerton kept her there. No one could move her.

Elizabeth languished, with periodic fits, for three years, and finally died. Two days before she died a neighbour visited her and asked her how she was. She replied that she could not speak about her condition because Deanes Gimmerton was sitting on her bed.

The outcome of Deanes Gimmerton's trial is not known.

[This piece was part of additional material written by Amanda Allsop and myself for Olive Knott's *Witches of Dorset*, 1974.]

LYTCHETT MATRAVERS [hamlet of HIGHER LYTCHETT]/LYTCHETT MINSTER

Lucky charm courtesy of the Celts

IF FARM workers found a discarded horseshoe they would nail it up, open end topwards, above a door. Similarly, a strange object lost or discarded in antiquity might also be regarded as having some potency as a charm.

A Victorian example, from Dorset, was the discovery in 1881 of a Celtic bronze statuette of a bull—one of their sacred cult animals—nailed over a door at Higher Lytchett, in the south-west corner of the parish of Lytchett Matravers. It had been found with other Iron Age scrap in the nearby hill-fort of Bulbury Camp—note the first bit, "bull-bury"—just over the boundary in the parish of Lytchett Minster [Ordnance Survey grid reference SY 928 942]. These earthworks are much denuded by ploughing.

When an antiquary, J. J. Foster, heard of the bull and followed its trail it led him to an old woman whose son had been sick: "My poor buoy, he wer turble bad, and he pined like a[f]ter they wold things. And ther—I thought myself how thick brass dog [using the word as it applies to any metallic object or tool, rather than failing to realise it is a bull] a noül'd ouver door'd do en a power o' good."

The son, obviously, must have improved. The bull has since been displayed in the Dorset County Museum at Dorchester.

NETHERBURY/BEAMINSTER/HALSTOCK

'Consorted with fairies'

ONE OF THE earliest cases of witchcraft in Dorset has as its victim John Walsh of Netherbury near Beaminster who was sent for trial in the 1560s. Walsh was said to have "consorted with white, green and black fairies who were cavorting on the hills of Dorset." He believed that these lived in prehistoric burial mounds.

The devil, said Walsh, "had a cloven hoof, and personally asked him to give a drip of blood each year—and a gift of two living things. Cats, dogs, and chickens were the devil's desire."

There is a contemporary record of John Walsh's interrogation, though I'll modernise the spellings to make its sense a little clearer. It is plainly a reference to prehistoric round barrow burial mounds. The nearest of these to Netherbury are on Beaminster Down [Ordnance Survey map reference ST 497 035]:

"He being demanded how he knoweth any man is bewitched, he sayeth that he knew it partly by the fairies, and sayeth that there be three kinds of fairies; white, green, and black. Which when he is disposed to use, he speaketh with them upon hills, where as there is great heaps of earth, as namely in Dorsetshire. And between the hours of twelve and one at noon, or at midnight, he useth them. Whereof, he sayeth, the black fairies be the worst."

No details survive of the poor man's fate but it seems clear he was cruelly tortured into making his confessions.

* * * * *

In the past hundred years there have occasionally been reminders that witchcraft is not totally forgotten in the isolated farmsteads and hamlets of the Marshwood Vale. Deep in the hills that skirt the Vale's western edge, in 1884 at a house in Hawkchurch on the Devon border, an obstruction was found lodged in the chimney. The building had been recently vacated by its tenant:

"The obstruction was got out, and was found to be neither brick nor stone, but a bullock's heart, with which stuck a quantity of the prickles of the white thorn, some nails, pins and other things."

A villager suggested that the former occupier, a bachelor, had possibly used the charm "to ward off the attacks of the ladies" and to prevent 'witches' from gaining access to the house via the chimney.

The previous year, 1883, an amazing story was reported from the countryside near Bridport. A dairyman's wife was induced by two 'strange women'—probably gipsies—into believing that money could literally 'breed' money. The gullible housewife gave them some sovereigns which the two women pretended to seal in a charmed sheep's heart with the warning that the heart was to remain secreted and unopened until Easter Sunday.

But the dairyman missed his money long before then, and the wife had to tell him that it was hidden away for a reason. He found in the chimney a smoked sheep's heart studded with pins in mystic patterns. Inside the heart were some bright, shining farthings.

Perhaps the superstitious would have said that the turning of the sovereigns into farthings was the penalty for breaking the spell. His wife believed they would have discovered "quite a happy family of new sovereigns and young half-sovereigns." Certainly, the two unknown women vanished the richer by several pounds.

As Reverend R. F. Meredith, rector of the west Dorset parish of Halstock, wrote to The Times in 1883: "There is no need to go to west Prussia for witchcraft. In a parish where the counties of Devon, Dorset and Somerset meet, a young man, being afflicted with scrofula which caused at times contraction of the muscles of the right thigh and very considerable pain, formed the idea that a poor delicate woman living next door, wife of a labourer and mother of several children, had bewitched him, and one day in his agony rushed into her house with a sewing needle, and before the woman had time to think, scratched her severely in the neck and in four places on her bare arm, drawing blood in each instance, then rubbed his hand on the blood and ran off. The poor woman came to me to complain, showing the scratches, and I advised her to take out a summons before the justices, but time passed. The young man, as usual, felt relieved of his pains for a time, and his mother, a widow occupying a few acres of land with her cows and pigs, tried to assure me that drawing the blood cured her son, for she considered the other woman had 'overlooked' him!"

Belief in witchcraft was widespread throughout west Dorset in the closing years of Victoria's reign. In 1884 the Bridport News gave the case of a woman, the wife of a woodman living in a parish towards Dorchester, who had been seriously ill for a long time. This woman was treated by a gipsy who told her she had been 'overlooked'.

The gipsy also informed her that she would never recover until the spell had been broken—something she said she could do for a small sum of money. The sick woman readily agreed and paid. She was then instructed by the gipsy to place certain flowerpots out of doors; when the flowers withered she would mend. The woman implicitly followed these and other instructions, and she recovered, as predicted, when the flowers drooped.

[This piece is based upon additional material written by me for Olive Knott's *Witches of Dorset*, 1974.]

SHERBORNE

'Sal Smith—I'll draw the blood of thee'

PUBLIC INTEREST in the Sherborne petty sessions of September 1884, was excited by a case arising out of alleged 'witchery' at Cold Harbour in the town's poor north-eastern quarter. The court was crowded with eager listeners who wanted to know the outcome of an incident on the 19th of that month.

Tamar Humphries, a married woman, was the defendant and she was accused of assault. The magistrates were told that she entered the garden of her next door neighbour, Sarah Smith—described as being "on the shady side of eighty"—and shook the old lady by her shoulders, saying: "Oh, Sal Smith, what's thee done to my child? You're a witch, and I'll draw the blood of thee."

Mrs. Humphries held a stocking needle in her hand and with this weapon "she made free use about the complainant's hands and arms."

Sarah Smith, questioned by the defence, said she had been the Humphries' neighbour for thirty years and that they had never quarrelled before. Sidney Watts, the defending lawyer, could only plead for his client that she had heard Sarah Smith "give her a bad name" and claim that the violence used amounted only to "a gentle shake." The defendant was in an upset state because her daughter was crippled with rheumatism.

The Bench took a more serious view of the garden blood-letting and considered

[This piece was part of the additional material written by me for Olive Knott's *Witches of Dorset*, 1974.]

it amounted to a disgraceful assault on an inoffensive old woman, who happened to be digging potatoes at the time. So they fined Tamar Humphries £1 with 11s 6d costs which in those days was more than a token penalty.

SHIPTON GORGE

Heart stuffed with pins

THOUGH I have read many third-hand accounts of pin-stuck hearts falling out of chimneys I have only once had the excitement of recording such an instance myself. It was in 1969, when looking back to about 1930, that Mrs. Muriel Aylott of Bournemouth told me about the discovery of one of these evil witch-charms at Shipton Gorge, to the north-east of Bridport:

"There was a chimney fire at Home Farm and when they were clearing the chimney of all the soot and debris they found a beam across and behind this beam, hanging on just one side, they found this heart. A pig's heart! It was all shrivelled and shrunk but it was stuck with pins. Extraordinary, it was.

"I don't know what happened to it. No. That was before I lived there. I lived in London when I was married and we just used to go down there for holidays and I know this heart was kept and shown to people."

SOUTH PERROTT

A community closed ranks for Jo

AMID ALL the persecution of so-called witches in the seventeenth century, there was one victim in a west Dorset parish who inspired a whole community to rise to her defence. The people of South Perrott were anxious to lay the potentially fatal rumours about Johane Guppie and banded together to issue the following statement which is set out here with its original spellings of the time:

"To all Christian people to whome this present certificate shall come wee the parishioners of South Perrott in the county of Dorset where Johane Guppie, the wiefe of Thomas Guppie, nowe dwelleth and of Stoke Abbott where the said Johane was born and of other parishes neere theer aboutes whose names are hereunder writen send greetinge in our Lord God. Know ye that wee the said parishioners and inhabitantes of the said places and thereabouts doe by theeis presentes signifie affirme and declare that the said Johane Guppie during all the time of her aboade and dwellinge in South Perrott aforesaid and before her coming theer hath did and doth behave herself in all things well and honestlye and never did to our knowledges or as we have ever heard eyther hurte or damage to anye person or persons whatsoever by waye of enchantmente sorcerye or witchcraft nor was ever accompted reckoned or knowen to be a woman that ever could use anye such thinge or to be a woman of the sorte condition or qualitie but contrariwise she hath donne good manye people aswell in curinge of dyvers peoples wounds and such like thinges as in drenchinge of cattell and such like exercises and alwayes hath lyved of good name and fame without anye spott or touch of enchantmente sorcerye or witchcraft. All which wee the parties hereunder named and menconed shall and wilbe alwayes readye to affirme and maynteyne whersoever and when wee shalbe called thereunto."

There follow the signatures of over twenty people.

[This piece was part of the additional material written by me for Olive Knott's *Witches of Dorset*, 1974.]

STALBRIDGE

A curse carried off the pigs

THE POWER of an Edwardian "wise woman" of Stalbridge was said to extend to man and beast alike. She was reputed to work in combination with a particularly old and repulsive bad-tempered hag who was known to drop the occasional curse into her business altercations. In one specific incident she was haggling over the purchase of some pigs from a neighbour.

Some of the animals were larger than the others and for these the neighbour stuck out for an extra shilling a piece. The hag refused to pay more than a set price and withdrew her offer completely. "Mark my words," she added. "They will never thrive with you."

In a fortnight all the pigs had died.

One year the villain of this story was herself very ill. In a dream she saw a supposed ill-wisher of hers—which could have included just about any of the neighbours—looking in through the window and laughing. Another "wise woman" was called in and between them the pair transferred the illness to the neighbour. The magic worked as the sick woman began to recover.

Olive Knott names two of the village's alleged dabblers in witchcraft, Mother Clinton and Old Biddy, in her *Witches of Dorset*, 1974, and adds:

"There seemed to be something in the very air of Stalbridge which fostered this belief in the black art. A person still living in the village can remember seeing an old woman sitting by her fireside, stabbing pins into a bullock's heart, muttering and mumbling as she flung it into the fire.

"Small wonder that bullocks' hearts have been found stuck in the chimneys of old Stalbridge houses, but strong as this belief was it has now completely died out. The villagers remember, but laugh away the stories of local witches."

TURNER'S PUDDLE

The clergyman convinced of witchcraft

REVEREND WILLIAM ETTRICK, an educated and unsuperstitious clergyman who was vicar of Affpuddle and Turner's Puddle at the beginning of the nineteenth century, suffered a series of misfortunes which completely converted his disbelief of the occult into a sincere fear of witchcraft. These misfortunes, occurring over a period of about a year, coincided with the arrival and presence of a particular servant at his vicarage in the tiny and lonely hamlet of Turner's Puddle on the edge of the heath near Bere Regis [Ordnance Survey map reference SY 830 935].

It took Mr. Ettrick a long time to come round to his eventual conviction that he was under an evil spell, but once he had, all seemed to confirm his suspicions. He kept a diary and recounted the curious and highly unpleasant events, all of which fit in with the movements of Susan Woodrow. She arrived at the house on 23 February, 1804, to work in the garden; she was renowned for her 'powers' with plants and vegetables, and Mr. Ettrick had employed her for that reason.

Four days after her arrival, Mr. Ettrick's horse—a young and healthy animal—fell sick. At this point he made no connection, though looking back later, he did. The horse apparently recovered.

Susan herself fell ill for a 'long time' and was away from the house until June. The day she came back, the same horse cut its foot and was lame for more than ten days. On 2 September, "the poor old horse caught a cold, and the Strangles." The animal worsened, catching other painful infections, until 16 September, when it died. Mr. Ettrick still did not suspect witchcraft and instead blamed the vet.

Four days later a pig was killed because it was ill. Mr. Ettrick now became suspicious. There was no apparent reason for the horse's sickness and death, nor that of the pig, and his dog had also died without cause. All medication to the animals had failed inexplicably. A horse he borrowed to fetch potatoes was also "very weak and seemingly going the way of mine by the vile witchcraft of a bad neighbour."

To add to his problems, all his children had fallen ill and the youngest was very ill indeed.

This youngest child, a boy, was born on 22 July, 1804. Susan Woodrow was at the house at the time and acted as nurse at the birth. She was the first to hold the new-born baby. From the moment of its birth, according to Mr. Ettrick, the child was in continual pain and torment. By November, after four months of constant anxiety and sleepless nights over his child, he connected this illness with the death of his horse. On 14 November, the day he borrowed his neighbour's horse, he writes: "I was once incredulous about the power of witchcraft, but have no doubts remaining." Of the child's illness, he writes: "It is like a demoniacal possession and began immediately after the child was snatched out of the mother's arms, by a hag reputed to be a witch."

This is the first indication that he suspected Susan. These suspicions continued and crystallised. He sent Susan away, and procured a phylactery which had been "inscribed with sacred words in the original character" and tied it round the child's body. The baby began to improve, and eventually seemed to have recovered completely.

But at the end of November, Susan returned to wash and perform various tasks. The child immediately sickened again. In his diary of 1 December, Mr. Ettrick directly accuses Susan Woodrow—according to him, she had often dropped expressions suggesting great pleasure at the child's sickness, and never once commiserated with its suffering or wished it better. Mr. Ettrick finally felt that as long as her connection with the house remainded, they would be under her power.

He decided to dismiss her, but did not actually do so until January 1805—and he then dismissed her as much for her impudence and deceit as for her witchcraft, of which he had openly accused her, giving it merely as one of the reasons for her dismissal.

Three days before he sacked her, he had a dream in which a strange, gruesome, black bird flew into the parlour where he was sitting and flew around him several times. It then perched upon his hat and he seized the bird, and with great difficulty wrung its neck, and then threw it to the floor. The cat, which was in the room, though eyeing the bird with a cat's natural eagerness, would not approach it.

It had taken the vicar a month to pluck up the courage to confront Susan and send her away. The dream seemed to have exorcised her evil influence and given him the courage to act.

Susan Woodrow, however, did not give up immediately. Three days later, on 7 January, she reappeared at the house with two letters from a neighbour which she had offered to deliver, presumably, or at least in Mr. Ettrick's opinion, to regain admission to the house and procure a fresh power there. But Mr. Ettrick refused to accept the letters from her and instead threatened her with a warrant for her removal if she would not leave willingly. After demanding to know from Mr. Ettrick what it was she was supposed to have done, she eventually left, though with great reluctance.

There is no further mention of the child in Etterick's diary, nor of further trouble. It seems that the child recovered and the family's misfortunes ceased. Mr. Ettrick never had enough substantial proof against her for any court charges—"her crime admits of no legal proofs, being all works of darkness." He does however list what he calls "The works of Susan" and it is for us to decide whether there was any witchcraft outside the paranoia of the vicar's own mind:

- the long and continued illness of the horse,
- the illness and death of a neighbour's horse,
- potatoes sorted by Susan and stored in the usual place were found rotten, whereas others less carefully stored were quite sound and good,
- the quarter of the garden dug by Susan had a succession of crop failures,
- the bees, which Susan had dealt with, had by the end of 1805 deserted their hives and left empty combs—Mr. Ettrick decided to keep no more bees.

[This account was part of the additional material written by Amanda Allsop and myself for Olive Knott's *Witches of Dorset*, 1974.]

WHITCHURCH CANONICORUM

'Belief in evil spirits prevalent into this century'

ELSEWHERE IN this section there has been evidence that the fear of witchcraft lasted as long as anywhere in the countryside around Bridport and in particular the Marshwood Vale. In all matters this area tends to be a couple of decades behind the rest of Dorset, for example in that several of its farms were still using horses in the 1950s and continued to thatch their ricks until the 1970s, and it was a backwater of superstitious belief. The evidence is provided by Sylvia Creed for her home parish of Whitchurch Canonicorum in *Dorset's Western Vale* which was published in 1987: "During renovations in one of the Manscombe buildings in the 1960s a bullock's heart stuck with thorns was found in a chimney breast. Witches were reputed to have been able to come down the wide old-fashioned chimneys so a bullock's heart was placed in a strategic position to deter such evil visitors. Several of these bullock hearts have been found in the area within living memory so belief in evil spirits and such like was prevalent well into this century."

We return to Whitchurch Canonicorum on pages 133-135 for the legends surrounding Saint Wite. These are hers: shrine, well, and church. She also puts in an appearance as a ghost on page 77.

Custom, that unwritten law,
By which the people keep even kings in awe.

— CHARLES DAVENANT [CIRCE]

Legend –
that in the crypt
beneath Milton Abbey
there is a coffin
full of stones.
See page 111.

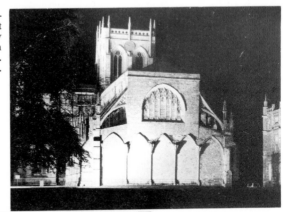

LEGENDS
AND
CUSTOMS

Custom –
Dorset's last
candle-auction,
taking place at Leigh.
See page 109.

The past is like another country,
they do things differently there.

— L. P. HARTLEY [THE GO-BETWEEN]

ABBOTSBURY

Legend of the Chesil Beach

THE FOLK explanation for the Chesil Beach, the great bank of pebbles that runs offshore for eight miles from Abbotsbury to Portland, is that it was washed up by the sea in a storm on a single night. The event is said to have happened after a pirate had fled into the creek at Abbotsbury after being chased by the King's vessels in about 1500.

Next morning he found himself floating in a lagoon and the royal fleet was out of sight on the high seas the other side of the Chesil Beach.

AFFPUDDLE [hamlet of BRIANTSPUDDLE]

T. E. Lawrence's mystery stone

IN 1934, T. E. Lawrence and Jock Chambers came across the Dead Woman's Stone which lay in a ditch beside the road across Throop Heath between Clouds Hill and Briantspuddle in the parish of Affpuddle [Ordnance Survey map reference SY 822 916]. Lawrence had heard that it marked the burial spot of a suicide who was buried beneath this crossroads at the extremity of the parish. He was intrigued by the stone and intended to move it nearer to Clouds Hill. It appealed to both the romantic and graver sides of the character of "Lawrence of Arabia" but nothing came of the plan because he died the following May after a motorcycle crash on the other side of Clouds Hill.

Jock Chambers returned after the war in search of the stone but found it gone and the spot heavily churned by tank tracks. He was told that it had been taken to a safe place by Canadian engineers. Later, at the age of seventy-five, Chambers came across it at last in the garden of a cottage near the school at Briantspuddle. The stone had indeed been moved, but not in the direction Lawrence intended—it was now a mile from Clouds Hill.

ALDERHOLT [hamlet of CRIPPLESTYLE]

The pilgrimage to King Barrow

WHEN THE mud-walled thatched chapel was built by Congregationalists among the remote heathland cottages of Cripplestyle, three miles west of Cranborne, the first pastor established a custom that was to last for a century and a half. William Bailey marched his flock from the chapel [Ordnance Survey map reference SU 091 122] and up the sandy track to the top of a gorse covered knoll known as King Barrow [map reference SU 094 123]. At the end of this fifteen minute procession, on the Thursday of Whit week in 1807, he hoisted a red flag, with the words "Feed my Lambs", on the summit and held an open air service of thanksgiving.

I researched the custom in 1970 and found that it had "still drawn a reasonable crowd of both young and old even in recent years. Because this annual pilgrimage has become more widely known, and a number of non-conformist churches in east Dorset wish to honour the Cripplestyle pioneers who built a chapel with their bare hands, there is every chance that the tradition will continue." The duty of carrying the flag fell to one of Bailey's descendants and the Thursday walk was for many years supported by Sunday school children from Verwood. They went back to a tea on the village green and many villagers remembered the clothes baskets that were filled with slab-cake. Chester cake, one of them called it, and described it as "middling between bread pudding and Christmas pudding".

For all that apparent interest it takes more than fruit-cakes to sustain a chapel. The roof was allowed to leak and the cob walls reverted to mud. In the late 1970s the Cripplestyle chapel collapsed. William Bailey had, after all, built upon sand.

BLANDFORD

Spoiling the stories of Wolfe and Wellington

TWO PERSISTENT Dorset traditions, which have been relayed to me as tenets of faith by many older people in the Blackmore Vale and Cranborne Chase, connect Wellington and Wolfe with the fields around Blandford. Unfortunately, in the form in which they are told, both stories are impossibilities. The commonest story, about James Wolfe, is that the army which sailed from Portsmouth in 1759 for the siege of Quebec was mustered and trained on the downs above the town.

The British Army did in fact converge upon what we know as Blandford Camp—then the town's racecourse—for a review of ten thousand soldiers, but that was three years earlier, on 31 August 1756. It was the start of the Seven Years War and amongst the troops was Lieutenant Colonel James Wolfe with the 20th Regiment of Foot from Devizes, and his father's regiment was also present. Their visit to Blandford has been telescoped by folk memory with that of the major event for which Wolfe jumped to fame and remembered as a single sequence.

The other nonsense is the belief that the Duke of Wellington inspected his troops at Blandford prior to the Battle of Waterloo. Here there is no excuse for the confusion. No one who had been alive at the time could have perpetrated it as everyone in the country knew that the bulk of the army and the Duke himself had been on the other side of the Channel from 1806 to 1814.

Still, folk beliefs have a life independent of book learning and verbal tradition has a strong and almost tribal hold on those to whom it is imparted. Wolfe and Wellington are probably here to stay.

The Giant who brings children

VICTORIAN DRAWINGS of the Cerne Giant hill-figure omitted its thirty feet of phallus and the prudery extended well into the twentieth century. His appearance in a water-colour on the dust-jacket of F. J. Harvey Darton's *English Fabric* was literally marred with a blue smear across the plates to avoid offending public taste. Similarly, recorded versions of his folklore are probably equally muted and the first appearance in 1893 of the belief that copulation whilst lying on the grass of the phallus would cure infertility does not mean it is not vintage stuff.

The psychological boost from sex on the Giant would be a fillip to any relationship. I know of one child who was conceived there. There is also anthropological evidence that in some tribal groups attitudes can act as a primitive contraceptive—suggesting that one's thoughts about the outcome may have some bearing on the matter.

The corollary is that the Cerne Giant doesn't like children; or rather that he likes them a little too much. Thomas Hardy heard that he eats babies, but similar fears were held of other ogres. The superstition was strongly attached to Napoleon. "They say that he lives upon human flesh and has rashers o' baby every morning for breakfast," a Hardy character says of the latter. "Baby, Baby, he will hear you as he passes the house, and he, from limb to limb will tear you, just as pussy tears a mouse."

In the 1986 guide to the Cerne Giant, entitled *Cerne's Giant and Village Guide*, I carefully analyse his Celtic origins and the conflicting claims that he might be either the Roman god Hercules or the native deity Cernunnos—which name would instantly account for those of the river and the valley settlements.

Here, as we are in realms of mystery and supposition, I can indulge other theories and mention that baby-killing attributes may be a shiver from the past that preserves the memory of human sacrifices. If the Cerne Giant is purely Celtic rather than Romano-Celtic he would date from a time when horrific three-dimensional figures appalled even the Romans who were quite at home with their own brutalities. Julius Caesar describes huge wickerwork figures ("immani magnitudine simular cra"), their limbs packed with living men and set ablaze. Such a Druidic sacrifice, if such horrors did in fact take place, would have looked as terrible on the Cerne Giant as anywhere—Helith burning men for the sun god, in the shape of a single mammoth being. A wickerwork construction of this type the Romans called a "kolosson" and as such practices were abolished, being to quote Strabo, "opposed to our usage," the imperial historians could only report them from the impressions left on folk memory.

An argument in favour of this theory is that it would give a role for the rectangular earthwork above the Giant's head that is called the Trendle. Into its palisaded enclosure the victims could have been herded to await the sacrifice. The Trendle is set on a noticeable slope rather than the nearby flat ground of the summit of the hill. This is an angle inconvenient for a building, so a "priest's house explanation" is unlikely, but it would make a compound of prisoners easier to guard. There is, as Professor Stuart Piggott points out in his book *The*

Druids, no excuse for ignoring the solid and reliable classical references to human sacrifices: "The Druids were the wise men of barbarian Celtic society, and Celtic religion was their religion, with all its crudities. It is sheer romanticism and a capitulation to the myth of the Noble Savage to imagine that they stood by the sacrifices in duty bound, but with disapproval in their faces and elevated thoughts in the minds."

Beltane, from the Gaelic *bealltuinn*, "blaze-fire", was the Celtic festival that welcomed spring. It would, given the fertility attributes of the Giant, be his time of year and the time when the hillside might be expected to come alive. Therefore one year a team of archaeologists camped up there to see if anyone came to pay their respects to Helith, to use his thirteenth century name that was recorded by Walter de Hemingford.

Tom Lethbridge describes the uneventful outcome in *Gogmagog* which was published in 1957: "Nearly twenty-five years ago now, a party consisting of three members of the Society of Antiquaries and a lecturer in anthropology made an expedition to Cerne to see if anything happened on Beltane. As youngest of the party, it fell to me to navigate the squad in the dark of night to a concealed place in the gorse bushes above the giant's head. We approached from the north and moved for some distance under what cover was available. It is most unlikely that our approach was observed. While three of the party slept in flea-bags, one kept watch. The night passed in quiet and without incident. The only tumult which greeted Helith was the wonderful dawn chorus of the birds."

The 180-feet high figure is cut into Giant Hill on the east side of the Cerne valley just north of Cerne Abbas village. There is a footpath from there, via the churchyard at the north end of Abbey Street, and you go left, through a gate in the wall that is topped by an inscription featuring a cherub that was rediscovered in 1986: "This Wall was Erected in 1838." Cross the field, over the dips that mark the site of the Benedictine Abbey that was here from 987 to 1539, to the stile beside the clump of beech trees. On the other side is a National Trust black-painted board about the Cerne Giant [Ordnance Survey map reference ST 667 017] and a path climbs the side of the hill. There is not, however, any public access into the Giant's sheep-pen at the time of writing and most visitors get no closer than Giant's View, a layby strategically sited beside the main road at the Sherborne end of the village.

CERNE ABBAS

Tails and other tales

DORSET'S PREMIER sacred well is in the churchyard at Cerne Abbas [Ordnance Survey map reference ST 666 013]. It has a strong flow and is kerbed with stones though until the seventeenth century it was a proper shrine "covered with a chapel dedicated to Saint Augustine". Villagers used to believe that apparitions could be seen in its water on Easter Sunday. It was also the practice for new-born babies to be brought to St Augustine's Well at sunrise to be dipped in its waters. Baptism was a pagan custom adopted by the Christians and here, with the proximity of the Cerne Giant hill-figure, one can feel an older religion.

"Folks hold to the belief," Henry Moule wrote in Victorian times, that the well "still works wondrous cures." It was also associated with the Dorset variant of the Kentish "long-tails" legend. The legend is that St Augustine, the "Apostle of the English" and first Archbishop of Canterbury—sent to Britain with forty monks by Pope Gregory in 596—gave tails to the wicked non-believers of Cerne Abbas.

Wilkinson Sherren detailed the tradition in his *Wessex of Romance* in 1908:

"There is a legend about St Augustine's connection with Cerne Abbas, however, which wears an air of probability in its account of the horseplay of some early Wessexmen, and but for the indignity offered to a holy man, it would verge on the realm of comedy. According to William of Malmesbury, the great prelate [Augustine] having converted Kent to the Christian faith, travelled over the rest of the English provinces as far as Ethlebert's dominions extended, and then visited Cerne Abbas.

"As a token of their mission, St Augustine destroyed the idol, Heil, and thereby dismayed and incensed its worshippers, who retired to plot their revenge. Meanwhile the company felt weary and thirsty and St Augustine stuck his staff into the ground and 'fetched out a crystal fountain'. Before the apostolic band could refresh themselves the inhabitants advanced, and with quite a modern appreciation of the power of ridicule, fastened the tails of cows to the garments of St Augustine and his companions, and drove them from the place.

"Wherefore, in punishment of this persecution, 'all the generation had that given them which they in contempt had fastened on these holy men'. General credence was given to the legend till 1774, and until that period the people of Cerne imagined the posterity of those who abused St Augustine still remained, and were distinguished by caudal appendages of moderate length."

There was a further legend at Cerne Abbas, recorded by Henry Moule, that two bare spots in the grass on the bank of the mill-stream to the west of Abbey Street marked the last footsteps of a man who had thrown himself in the water and drowned there.

CHRISTCHURCH

The puzzling epitaph

WE WERE NOT SLAYNE BVT RAYSD
RAYSD NOT TO LIFE
BVT TO BE BVRIED TWICE
BY MEN OF STRIFE
WHAT REST COVLD TH LIVING HAVE
WHEN DEAD HAD NONE
AGREE AMONGST YOV
HEERE WE TEN ARE ONE
HEN: ROGERS DIED APRILL 17. 1641

THE CRYPTIC epitaph to Henry Rogers — and, it implies, nine others who are now counted as one—has kept its secret well. Some of the theories offered in explanation are more bizarre than the original wording which is cut into the side of a table-tomb in the churchyard of Christchurch Priory. One offering is that they were the victims of a shipwreck who were initially buried in the sand on the beach—but that ignores the first two lines and the context of the period.

This would be seen in the 1640s as a Civil War innuendo. At the beginning of the contest between king and Parliament came the impeachment of Thomas Wentworth, first Earl of Strafford, who was to lose his head on Tower Hill on 12 May 1641. "Men of strife" is a loaded phrase. Christchurch was a puritan town and "Men of strife" is a reference to the king's soldiers. It has its parallel in the nickname that the puritans reserved for the king—"Man of blood".

"Not slaine but raised" is also explicit enough, given the events of the decade—they were hanged rather than put to the sword. The word "raised" is then used again to describe their subsequent unearthing and re-burial. There would have been a general distaste and superstitious resistance to the disturbance of the dead.

"Here we ten are one" has to be interpreted in the light of an exhumation. By the time they were reburied the collection of bones were probably jumbled into a single coffin.

All that leaves is the mystery itself. Who were Henry Rogers and his friends, and why were they hanged on 17 April 1641?

DURWESTON

Ancient custom of Shroving

DURWESTON, TO the north of Blandford, is the only Dorset village that has maintained its ancient shroving custom without any real break. Children roam through the village on Shrove Tuesday shroving for pancakes and sweets and singing the traditional rhyme:

> I be come a shroven
> For a piece of pancake
> Or a bit of bacon
> Or a little truckle cheese
> Of yer own maken
> Blow the fire
> He't the pan
> For I be come a shroven.

In most years the press rediscovers the custom and the oldest villagers recall their shroving experiences of decades ago. For instance, in 1963, the folk memory went back to the time of Queen Victoria's Diamond Jubilee, to 1897, when Mr Lucas learnt the rhyme. Two other elderly men, T. Adlem and S. Tapper, remembered shroving in Edwardian times.

That the custom has survived to the present day is thanks to the practical concern of Valentine Rickman who left, when he died in 1925, the sum of £50 to a trust so that shroving money could be paid out by the rector in the church porch—asking that the interest "should be divided as evenly as possible between the children; share and share alike".

FOLKE

Supernatural transport

THERE WAS a legend at Folke, a tiny village south-east of Sherborne, that the parish church [Ordnance Survey map reference ST 660 133] was originally being built a mile to the south in Broke Wood [map reference ST 662 120] but the foundations were supernaturally moved during the night to the present location.

It is a belief typical of parishes where the church has been re-located after a shift of population; perhaps to justify divine approval for the move. In the case of Folke this sort of relocation is very likely to have happened as Broke Wood, though now completely unpopulated, is much nearer the centre of the parish than the site which is occupied by the mediaeval church.

FRAMPTON

The curse against the first-born

GOD'S CURSE against those who fortuned from the dissolution of the religious houses in 1539 was said to be that no first-born son of the rising rich, the families who moved into intact monastic buildings, would live to inherit the estate. There is one of these legends associated with Frampton Court [Ordnance Survey map reference SY 625 947], near Maiden Newton. It is on the site of a Benedictine priory.

Nature or God anyway loads the odds against the first-born, literally in that they are the eldest, and in the nation's premier family it has not been uncommon for the crown to pass to the Duke of York, the traditional title bestowed upon the second son.

In the case of Frampton its tradition is recorded in the Westminster Gazette for January 1918:

"There is a legend connected with Frampton Court that a monastery stood on the site of the present house, and when King Henry VIII sequestrated its lands and dwellings the Abbot pronounced a curse upon it that the eldest son of its possessor should never live to inherit its domains. So far no first born son has lived to succeed his father."

GUSSAGE ST MICHAEL

Legend was put to the test – and found lacking, to the incredulity of the yokels, in this ancient burial mound above the Gussage valley.

No golden coffin

WHEN STUART PIGGOTT and his team of excavators from the Royal Commission on Ancient Monuments began digging a Neolithic period oval-shaped barrow on

Thickthorn Down, above Gussage St Michael in the foothills of Cranborne Chase, they were constantly asked if they had yet discovered the golden coffin. Not only was there no gold, however, but Piggott's excavation in 1933 found nothing else either of what should have been the primary interments in the 5,000-year-old mound [Ordnance Survey map reference ST 972 123].

The barrow may have been a cenotaph for a warrior who was killed elsewhere. All that was left by the original builders were a couple of chalk-cut phallic objects which were found in the lowest layer of silting in the ditch which flanked the mound. Hundreds of years later the mound had been dug into and re-used for three other burials. Piggott and the locals were equally puzzled that it had been built to cover nothing whatever; the story of the golden coffin stuck tenaciously until the site had been completely cleared. The mound was reconstructed when the excavation had finished.

A similar golden coffin legend is associated with a group of ancient burial mounds near Milborne St Andrew.

HALSTOCK

Thomas Hollis –
a great mind
who has left
us legends
and saw
in the United
States of America
his libertarian dream.

Buried with his horse

LEGEND AT Halstock maintains that an eccentric eighteenth century landowner, who is remembered across the Atlantic as the principal philanthropist in the endowment of Harvard University Library, is buried beside his favourite horse. The animal was killed after its master had died on 1 January 1774 and they were lowered into a ten feet deep grave in the middle of a field at the appropriately named Harvard Farm, above the Dorset corner of Sutton Bingham Reservoir [Ordnance Survey map reference ST 550 095].

The disposal of his body followed the strict instructions that he had left: "The field should be immediately ploughed over and no trace of his burial place might remain."

He had attached himself to no religion and his sole spiritual opinion was that people had an immutable right to hold any religious belief that they wished—or none. He was a rationalist who had emerged from an age of unreason and he saw the fight for a free society that was taking place in Britain's north American colonies as the major contemporary world event that had the potential to advance the human mind. This Dorset man was mentally one of the first Americans.

Hollis left his mark firmly on the landscape of north-west Dorset with a habit of naming farms and fields after the places and people he admired.

Locke Farm, near Halstock, was a tribute to the philosopher, and the enclosures Reasonableness, Understanding and Comprehension were taken from his works. Appropriately, though, it is the Halstock farm he named Harvard which was going to become Hollis's grave.

Harvard Farm was 211 acres and sixth in size on the list of Hollis properties. It was the one he was personally managing at the time of his death and it abounds with echoes of colonial places and politics—parcels of land called New England, Boston, Mayhew, Cotton, Massachusetts, Hutchinson, Belchier, Eliot, Adams,

Revolution, William III, Settlement, Hanover and Stuart Coppice. Massachusetts tenuously retains its name, in a clipped way. The farmhands now call it "Massy Field".

The nomenclature convincingly sets the date of the farm's layout at 1773 when Hollis was absorbed with feeling for the "friends of liberty". That was the key word; there is a Liberty Farm. Hollis realised that the deteriorating colonial administration was driving New England towards its revolutionary war. He warned William Pitt, the Earl of Chatham, that the people of New England were "the first people upon earth for plain sense and virtue" and the present intention was to "humble and destroy them". Britain's Prime Minister was stinging the "people of New England into madness". Hollis asked: "What wonder that they should throw themselves upon their and our tutelary to save colonies and country, liberty, the principle of the Revolution, and, against itself, the House of Hanover."

If, in the tithe maps and documents, any Dorset historian comes across the original names of some of the seven hundred acres owned by Hollis, some attention must be taken of their situation and condition before assuming the naming is a gesture of admiration. Archbishop Thomas Secker appears on a map with an enclosure to his name, but as Hollis named this particular field in the 1760s this "most probably underlines disapprobation" as the churchman aroused Hollis's indignation by campaigning to send a bishop to America.

HOLNEST

Archetypal mad squire

The
Drax
Mausoleum.

IT HAS taken less than a century for the story of "Squire Holnest" to degenerate through its folk-lore stage into a version that is fake-lore. "One of the Squires of Charborough was called Holnest," Kingsley Palmer's informant writes in *Oral Folk-Tales of Wessex* [1973]. His account is then basically correct but the first fact isn't. He wasn't "Squire Holnest"—he was Squire Drax; full name John Samuel Wanley Sawbridge Erle Drax. The "Silent MP" he was called; because he had allegedly spoken only once in the House of Commons and then to ask if a window might be opened.

The confusion in the names arose because he moved from Charborough, northwest of Poole, to Holnest Park [Ordnance Survey map reference ST 653 090], four miles south of Sherborne. To the family his nickname was "Sawbridge" and over the years I have collected many stories about him.

He had a mock-Byzantine style mausoleum built in Holnest churchyard [map reference ST 656 098], between the ancient church and the main road, and even rehearsed his own funeral. He shouted curses every time they jogged his body. Arrangements were made for the daily delivery of The Times after he had moved into permanent occupancy.

The memorial stone was also carved in advance, leaving a space for the line that was to contain the date. It would be 5 January 1887; at the age of eighty-six. The Dorset County Chronicle reported: "The cortège was of considerable length, being headed by two mutes, followed by Messrs. Clarabut and Son of Wye, undertakers; then the body enclosed in an oak shell, a lead coffin, and outer coffin of oak grown on the Holnest estate and made by Mr. Long of Sherborne nearly three years ago.

"The coffin was conveyed in a handsome car with glazed sides and drawn by four magnificent black horses; twelve men employed on the Holnest estate acted as bearers. The coffin was placed in a kind of brass chest with a heavy cover. The mausoleum in which Mr. Drax's remains are deposited was built some fifteen years ago. It is a handsome building as large as many a small chapel."

* * * * *

No one of that generation would forget Drax and numerous stories were handed down to the next. Edwin Short [1884–1974] was born at Hilfield below the beech-covered slopes of High Stoy [which he called "High Sty"] and his father was a builder who did work for the local squires. Inevitably, these had included Drax, and in 1973 Mr Short recalled for me some of the stories that he had heard in his childhood: "My father worked for Drax who was a queer sort of old man, though good in a way. People wouldn't put up with him today, you know. Workmen couldn't then—he never thought of paying them a weekly or even a monthly wage. My father had to wait eleven months for his money.

"Anybody from there could go into the shops at Sherborne and say: 'We work for Holnest Estate, so we can't pay you.' They would be given credit. After the eleven months my father needed his money and said to the estate steward: 'If you don't mention it to the squire then I will do so myself.'

"Father accosted Squire Drax one morning and said: 'I want some money. The baker won't call any more as we owe him £22 for bread.' Drax wrote him out a cheque for the full amount on the spot and sent his postboy into Sherborne to cash it.

"That had its good side and its bad side, for it made people dishonest. If people had twelve months' money they had a good spree and wouldn't pay other people. Stickland, who lived at Holnest Lodge, was the head mason working with my father. He disappeared for a long time after he was paid.

"This Drax would spend money foolishly. He had a huge picture gallery built on Holnest House and thought nothing of going to Christie's in London and outbidding Queen Victoria for a painting. He is reputed to have earned £45,000 a year from all his estates but he couldn't live on it. In the last few years of his life he inherited another £15,000 and said he could just about rub along now. But he died in debt and the whole estate was under trustees for twenty-one years. The heir had no more control over it than you or I and it was let to a family by the name of Drake. They occupied Holnest till the first world war and then sold out. I went and bought a couple of pictures—one was called 'The blind fiddler' and the other 'The rent day'."

The picture gallery has since been pulled down and the other relics of Drax are gone: "The road leading into Holnest Park was stuck with images all the way up. Some went to Weymouth and are still there in the gardens. The mason at the lodge, who worked for Drax, could mould anything."

Drax also employed a man to walk round his house day and night to shout the state of the weather with cries like "sunshine," "star-light" or "rain coming." The park at Holnest was covered with buffalo and deer. It was fenced by high iron palings with spiked tops. Sometimes an animal would try to leap the fence and impale itself: "I remember eating some buffalo. It was given out and my father brought home a nice joint. It was as good as any beef."

The architectural masterpiece of the Drax mausoleum was demolished in 1935. Workmen with sledgehammers and picks tore up the mosaic paving and stones which had been cut by Edwin's uncle, John Short, in the 1870s. The embalmed body was buried under a marble memorial tablet which became the gravestone. No clergyman or member of the family attended the reburial.

IWERNE COURTNEY [or SHROTON as it is commonly known]

The Bull Pit on Cranborne Chase

BULL BAITING was a popular mediaeval blood sport and bull pits were used for the tethering of the animals when they were not being baited. Few of these pits have survived and I have only come across one in Dorset. It is on the Cranborne Chase uplands on the west side of the Higher Blandford Road to the south of the crossroads above Iwerne Minster [Ordnance Survey map reference SU 887 134] in a wood that I later found was tellingly called Bull Pit Coppice. It is very much private and determinedly fenced against any public access.

The circular pit is ninety feet across and seven feet deep. A sunken track curves round the outside of the pit from the south-west to a ramped opening in the north-east side of the pit. A clump of spruce trees stand in the pit and it is surrounded by a hazel thicket.

The dimensions and details of this pit correspond with those found by Somerset historian Robin Atthill on the Mendip Hills. Bull pits are described in the reference books as being generally located in towns or big villages but the Mendip examples and this one I have found in the parish of Iwerne Courtney are in open country and apparently deliberately placed far away from habitation.

LEIGH

Candle-auctions flickering out

IN 1972 I DID my bit to save Dorset's last remaining candle-auction. It was held in the King's Arms, near the bridge in the Blackmore Vale village of Leigh, from before 1800 until the closure of the inn in 1926. The event was transferred to the tiny village school. Then in 1972, landlord John Robbins of the Carpenter's Arms, now the village's only pub, invited parish council chairman Frank Goldsack to hold the auction there. An official notice was issued: "The annual candle-auction will be held at the Carpenter's Arms, Leigh, at 8 p.m. on Tuesday, 26 September. The old custom of a free whisky per bid will be revived by courtesy of the landlord."

On the 25th this notice was obliterated: "Cancelled by chairman of parish council, F. Goldsack."

He had responded to objections that it was unlawful to hold such an event in licensed premises. I obtained an opinion from Bournemouth solicitor Ian McQueen to the effect that Leigh's councillors had hastily acceded to a lie— indeed property auctions all over the country are held in public houses.

The auction returned, however, to the schoolroom, on 29 September [Michaelmas Day] when the two tenancies involved actually started. Eighteen people came and the first candle drowned in its wax, leaving almost all the eighth of an inch slither unburnt and Bill Notley with the 9.5 acres of Alton Mead for the bargain price of £11.   It was recalled that the same meadow had gone for £36 in 1952.

For Bere Mill Mead, only an acre and a half, the second candle lasted more than fifteen minutes but R. M. Austin's £5.50 bid seemed to hang in the air for an age before J. Webber spluttered "Six pounds" with perfect timing as the light died.

George Wallis, a council roadman, told me that the auction money used to be divided out for a loaf of bread, a pound of tea, and ten shillings for the poor at Christmas.   As a boy he had attended a pre-1926 auction at the King's Arms: "This now is a storm in a teacup about where it's held.   It is an old tradition and it ought to be carried on; a real old tradition, just before Sherborne's Pack Monday Fair.   Some crafty sod's come in trying to stop it, and that'll be an old tradition gone."

Candle-auctions provided a means by which a community could hire out its assets virtually by lottery—an unpredictable flame gave under-bidders a chance and prevented the wealthy from always monopolising the show.

LYDLINCH [hamlet of KING'S STAG]

White Hart Silver

THERE IS, it seems, no documentary evidence for the payment to the State of "White Hart Silver" as a fine by successive owners of land at King's Stag bridge in the Blackmore Vale [Ordnance Survey map reference ST 727 103].   Legend says it was imposed for the killing of a hind that Henry III [king from 1216 to 1272] had spared whilst hunting in this royal forest.   It is a good story and it does have the perfect pedigree, being first recorded by Thomas Gerard in his *Survey of Dorsetshire* of the 1620s, which was published in 1732 under the name of John Coker, the earliest book devoted to the county.   He writes:

"From Mapowder [Mappowder] the Brooke [River Lydden] passeth through deepe and dirtie Soyle under *King's Stagge Bridge*, which got that Name upon this Occasion: King Henry the Third, haveing disported himselfe in the Forrest of *Blackmore*, he spared one beautiful and goodlie white Harte, which afterwards *T. de la Linde*, a neighbour Gentleman of antient Descent and especiall Note, with him Companions pursueing, killed at this Place; but hee soone founde howe dangerous it was, to bee twitching a Lion by the Eares: For the King tooke soe great Indignation against him, that hee not onlie punished them with Imprisonment and a grievous Fine of Money, but for this Fact hee taxed their Lands; the Owners of which ever sithence yearlie untill this Daye paye a rounde Summe of Money by waye of Amercement unto the Exchequer, called *White Harte Silver*; in Memorie of which this C------- [calumny] needeth noe better Remembrance, than the annuall Payment.   The Posteritie of this Man ever after gave for their Armes, *White Hartes Heads in a red Shielde*; when as formerlie they gave the Coat of *Hartly*, whose Heire they had married: And the Forrest allsoe from that time beganne to lose its antient Name, and to bee called the *Forrest of Whiteharte*."

In this extract I have modernised the long-s [f] into a normal-s but otherwise the contemporary spellings have been retained.   Gerard laments the dropping of the old name of Blackmore but it has now totally reasserted itself and the charming Whitehart Vale alternative is now completely extinct.

MELCOMBE HORSEY/CHESELBOURNE

Stones that move at cock-crow

IN 1866, Canon C. W. Bingham recorded a popular tradition about two sarsen stones close to the prehistoric Giant's Grave burial mound at the foot of a hillside south of Hartfoot Lane, in the centre of the county [Ordnance Survey map reference ST 758 017]: "There is a long mound in a part of my parish which is popularly called the Giant's Grave, and very near two large stones which have probably rolled down from the beds of chert-like rock on the side of the chalk hill above. I discovered lately that there is a popular tradition existing—though my informant somewhat doubts its correctness—that these stones move whenever they hear the cocks crowing in Cheselbourne, a neighbouring village."

Cheselbourne is a mile away down the valley. Giant's Grave is immediately below the west side of Henning Hill; the name of which is given as Hanging Hill by Charles Warne, the antiquary, who added to the mythology associated with Giant's Grave: "Two giants standing on Norden [an adjacent hill—Nordon Hill, Melcombe Horsey, map reference ST 750 031] were once contending for the mastery as to which of them would hurl the farther, the direction being across the valley to Hanging Hill. He whose stone fell short was so mortified at the failure, that he died of vexation and was buried beneath the mound which has since been known as the Giant's Grave."

MILBORNE ST ANDREW

Lightning when they dig

A GOLDEN coffin is said to be buried in one of the three prehistoric round barrows on the Cowleaze, a former pasture half a mile south-east of the village [Ordnance Survey map reference SY 811 967].

Thunder and lightning begins if anyone starts to dig for it, members of the Women's Institute were told when they recorded village folklore in the 1930s.

MILTON ABBAS

The coffin full of stones

FREDERICK FANE glanced nervously over the assembled meeting as he prepared to deliver his speech to the learned body. He hesitated at the start of his notes and apologised humbly for bringing a trivial and frivolous matter to their attention.

The setting was a gathering at Dorchester of the Dorset Natural History and Antiquarian Field Club in 1895. I wrote this account under the pseudonym Gareth Gwynne, for one of the first issues of the Dorset County Magazine in 1968, to conceal a shortage of contributors.

Fane's story concerned stones so he decided geology might be an appropriate "ology" for the talk. He started with recollections of a pheasant shooting stay at Milton Abbey in the October of 1873. Breakfast was late one morning and Fane strolled into the abbey church where repairs were being carried out on the north transept.

There he talked with the clerk of works who told the history of Milton Abbas. How, one hundred years before, the village clustered about its abbey. The owner, Lord Milton, tired of the cottaged surround and replaced it with a flower garden. He achieved a view from the windows of his house by transplanting the community in a hidden coombe—the present Milton Abbas.

Just before the resiting of the village, a young Damer, son of Lord Milton, embarrassed the family by his extravagance and owed considerable sums. Bailiffs searched Milton for the elusive debtor.

This set the scene for Fane's strange story. The clerk of works told him that one day a message arrived at Milton saying young Damer had died on the continent and his body was being returned for burial. A coffin was brought to the village and taken at a grandiose funeral to the vaults below the abbey.

No more was heard from the anxious creditors—but the villagers were sure they kept seeing young Damer, in the flesh, about his paternal home.

Fane continued: "Standing in conversation by the monument to Lord Milton, the clerk told me that, for underpinning, it had been necessary to open and examine the flooring of the transept. In doing so they had come upon the entrance of the Milton vaults."

The clerk invited Fane to go below. They passed two considerable open vaults, with numerous coffins upon tressels, some covered with tattered velvet and pasteboard coronets lying on their tops. In the farthest vault was a coffin, with brass nameplate which had been attached to the outer case, still lying on the minor leaden one. The inscription detailed the name of a Damer who died at little more than twenty years somewhere about 1770.

"Now, sir, try to lift that coffin as it lies on the tressels," said the clerk.

"This I found impossible, owing to its extraordinary weight," Fane told the meeting.

"Now try to lift this one," said the clerk as he pointed to another coffin.

"Up it came without the slightest exertion," Fane commented.

Explained the clerk: "This one contains a body gone to dust—the other is full of stones, as was supposed by the old villagers."

The clerk was happy: he had proved a village legend to the satisfaction of an outsider and a gentleman. Historians at the meeting were staggered—they had heard the oddest paper ever read to the Dorset Field Club. Discussion followed and the Rev. G. Bridges Lewis of Broadstone mentioned the tomb at St. Albans of Duke Humphrey. The body was preserved in spirit but so many tasted the liquor that the corpse was left dry. Coach travellers visited the tomb, during the time allowed for a meal at the inn, and coined a phrase: "To dine with Duke Humphrey."

MORDEN/CHARBOROUGH/WAREHAM ST MARTIN

Last wild boar in England

THERE SEEMS to be reasonable evidence for the local claim that the woods at Morden Park, around a lake on the heath, contained the last herd of wild boar in

England. They were not, however, mediaeval survivors but continental specimens—a pair from Russia and a pair from France—that the eccentric owner, John Samuel Wanley Sawbridge Erle Drax, had released in about 1840. The Russians proved to be wilder and more ferocious than the French, which should not have surprised anyone of the post-Napoleonic generation. Drax killed them off when it became clear that they would start escaping into the surrounding countryside.

Drax wrote about them in 1879: "I fenced them in with a wood paling in the wood where I built the present tower [Charborough Tower, Ordnance Survey map reference SY 929 976], and used to shoot them. The latter part of the time I kept them at Morden Park [map reference SY 907 930], and bred a lot of them, feeding them on turnips and corn. They were savage and troublesome, however, to keep within bounds, and I therefore killed them. They were good eating when fed upon corn."

The Drax reintroduction was later than that made by Sir Francis Darwin into his woods in Derbyshire. The last of those animals was shot in 1837. As for the genuine wild boar, the indigenous sort, they survived at Chartley until after 1683. The best description of tracking the "Wyld Bore" is by a Dorset gentleman, George Turbervile, in his *Booke of Hunting* (1575).

"Doth the old boar feed in the old frank?" Shakespeare asks in *Henry IV*, part two. The frank was the pen in which boars used to be confined and fattened. I have long hoped to come across a Dorset reference to a "boar-frank" though for the time being I'll be satisfied with my vigorous Romano-British statuette of a wild boar. It is a beast par excellence—the premier sacred animal of the Celts.

PIMPERNE/PRESTON

The soldiers who showed what the Turks had done to them

WHILST TRACING the steps of Charles Kingsley's Dorset courtship, to prepare material in 1974 for the author's centenary year, I had a chance encounter with Pimperne's affable rector, Rev. D. A. Farquharson-Roberts. He talks history with ease and casually mentioned a link between his present and previous Dorset parishes. When he was a curate at Preston, near Weymouth, he came across an early nineteenth century record of a visit to the parish by four British soldiers who had been captives of the Turks.

"They revealed their mutilations," the rector said. He immediately clarified this statement in a way not so entirely inappropriate for one who is also an ex-officer of the Royal Marines: "In other words they showed where their balls had been cut off! The note shows that they were given 2s 6d each from the fund for parish poor."

When he came to Pimperne, which has its records intact from Tudor times, Mr. Farquharson-Roberts found that history is repetitive. In the same month, the same number of ex-prisoners of the Turks had arrived there too, exhibited themselves, and received half-a-crown each. It is more than probable that they were the same people but the people of Pimperne must also have been aware that they were viewing a travelling circus and were prepared to pay the market price for their peep show.

The incident is an indication that the effectiveness of British foreign policy in Asia Minor has always been precarious. Historically, Britain has either been on very good terms, or alternatively appalling terms, with the Turks depending on whether we were currently in alliance with the Russians. Britain in league with Russia meant acquiescence in their hostilities against Turkey, or even in active participation. This was the position through most of the eighteenth century but Pitt changed the policy—to restrain Russian ambitions—and the Turks were then our friends.

The understanding soon ended. France intervened and in 1807 a British expeditionary force landed at Constantinople to castigate the Turks for their treaty with Napoleon. The British invaders failed disastrously and it may be from this defeat that the castrated soldiers returned. The Government may have approved of their public exhibition as visual proof that Britain had been beaten by no normal enemy.

PIMPERNE

The last pillory in Dorset

THERE IS at Pimperne a survival from a brutal past. Outside the churchyard [Ordnance Survey map reference SU 904 095], underneath a great horse chestnut tree beside the village street, is the substantial platform and stump of a mediaeval preaching cross, constructed of large greensand blocks. They are heavily weathered and came somewhere from the line of quarries in the hillsides on the north edge of Cranborne Chase, between Tisbury and Shaftesbury.

On the south-east corner of the steps is a deep heel-shaped scoop. The rector, Rev. D. A. Farquharson-Roberts, explained its significance to me: "I've seen an old picture of 1906 showing a wooden pillory standing next to the cross. It was so close that the poor felons used to stick out their left foot for support on this stone, and that wore this hole deep into it."

The pillory was a punishment of confined standing with the offender's head and hands fastened through the holes of its wooden frame. The severity of the punishment depended on the reaction of the public. The victim was entirely at their mercy, as he was powerless to attempt any defence, and his face could be pulped out of recognition by the determined throwing of rubbish and brickbats. Until 1637 it was principally used for offences that we would regard as those of consumer protection but Parliament then extended its use into the realm of press censorship. Pamphleteers who attacked the Government were pilloried. Daniel Defoe, who had fought for Monmouth in the 1685 Western Rebellion, became the satirist of his age and appeared in the pillory in 1702. For a few political offenders their time in the pillory was a triumph. They were protected by admirers and smiled through a cascade of rose petals.

No one went into the pillory after the Napoleonic Wars and it was legally abolished in 1837. Several pillories survive in England but, after the removal of Pimperne's, there is none in Dorset.

PORTESHAM/
PORTLAND

Like the Agglestone at Studland, the Hell Stone(s) was thought to have fallen from the sky. Both names may have originally been the same – hailstone.

Hell Stone and the devil's game

THE PLAYING of quoits—the pitching of a ring over a pin set in the ground—was popular enough in mediaeval times to warrant condemnation in Acts of Parliament that tried to limit the popular games that were distracting young men from practising archery at the butts. Folklore associates the game of quoits and the devil with an impressive megalithic monument on the downs between Portesham Hill and the Hardy Monument [Ordnance Survey map reference SY 606 868]. Its sarsen stones are said to have been thrown by the devil whilst he was playing quoits on Portland.

The Hell Stone, as the monument is known, is a Neolithic burial chamber dating from before 3,000 BC. It was formerly covered by a mound of earth, over ninety feet long, but this is now reduced to a small hump only five feet high and it is crossed by the stone wall of a far more recent field boundary.

Charles Warne, the Victorian antiquary, described the burial chamber as a collapsed cromlech:

"The supports of the capstone have sunk on the south-west side, and are virtually buried by it, its great weight being now chiefly sustained by a single prop on the north side, so that it rests in a greatly-inclined position. It measures more than ten feet in length, about seven feet in breadth, and has an average thickness of at least two feet and a half. Originally it must have rested upon eight or ten supports. No doubt it was devoted to sepulchral purposes and in its original state was probably covered with a mound of earth."

It now looks much more splendid than that, thanks to a fanciful rebuilding carried out by Rev. Martin Tupper—the author of *Proverbial Philosophy* which went through dozens of editions and sold more than a million copies in America. He lived at Albury, near Guildford.

The "initiatory restoration" of the Hell Stone was completed on 11 June 1866 when Martin Tupper, J. V. W. Vandelour, John Nichols, H. de Beauvoir Tupper, Robert Gambier Sweeting, John Bull and W. K. Tupper posed for a photograph. The team, however, had failed to replace the huge capstone on top of the burial chamber.

Eight Portland quarrymen arrived on 14 August 1869 to finish the job. They brought screw-jacks and succeeded in raising the sixteen-ton oval capstone on to the top of the nine supporting pillars. The men did their job well as the capstone has stayed in its new position for more than a century without shifting an inch.

Nearby, another probable Neolithic burial chamber was less fortunate in the attention it received in the mid-nineteenth century. Its stones, which stood in the field immediately north-west of Black Down Barn [Ordnance Survey map reference SY 607 870], were completely broken up by farm workers. Their sizes and layout were encompassed in a delightful anthropomorphic name: "Jeffrey and Joan, their little dog Denty, with Eddy alone."

PORTLAND

Courting customs

INSULAR PORTLAND, that hump jutting incongruously into the English Channel, first earned reputation by selling itself. Outsiders came through the flourishing stone trade to Portland—and were surprised to find the islanders almost a separate breed, a race of natives clinging to a code of morals long forgotten elsewhere.

Their marriage customs are quaintly divulged by a London printer in a manner which, although outwardly the style of the late eighteenth century, comes near to a modern mass newspaper or sociological study in its approach. This account I wrote under the name Ross Brown for an early issue of Dorset County Magazine in 1968—when pseudonyms disguised a lack of contributors.

John Smeaton, builder of the third Eddystone lighthouse, completed in 1759, visited the quarries of Portland and had as guide a Mr. Roper. He told Smeaton of a local love custom which ensures compatibility by not allowing marriage until the girl is pregnant.

Though the custom sounds to us to be too close to free love to have been the basis of morality, in a closed society highly coloured by tradition, I am sure that Portland is unique only in being the example which was recorded. Certainly the withdrawn and inbred nature of the place helped the way of life from another age to survive intact. Similarities exist with the then current American practice of bundling and before the imposition of moral ethics this must have been habitual everywhere. "Portland custom" it was called—which is shorter than attempting the explanation in current phraseology.

Smeaton admired the strength and healthy looks of the Portland men, and the ease with which they operated in the quarries. He asked Roper where "they could possibly pick up such a set of stout hardy fellows".

Roper: If you knew how these men are produced you would wonder the less for all our marriages are productive of children.

Smeaton: Can you give an explanation of how this happens?

R: Our people here, as they are bred up to hard labour, are very early in a condition to marry and provide for a family. They intermarry with one another, very rarely going to the mainland to seek a wife and it has been the custom of the Isle, from time immemorial, that they never marry till the woman is pregnant.

S: But pray, does not this subject you to a great number of bastards? Have not your Portlanders the same kind of fickleness in their attachments, that Englishmen are subject to and in consequence, does not this produce many inconveniences?

R: None at all, for previous to my arrival here, there was but one child on record of the parish register, that had been born a bastard, in the compass of 150 years. The mode of courtship here is that a young woman never admits of the serious addresses of a young man, but on the supposition of a thorough probation. When she becomes with child, she tells her mother; the mother tells her father; and he tells the boy, that is then the proper time to be married.

S: But suppose, Mr. Roper, she does not prove with child, what happens then—do they live together without marriage, or, if they separate, is not this such an imputation upon her, as to prevent her getting another suitor?

R: The case is thus managed.   If the woman does not prove with a child, after a competent time of courtship, they conclude they are not destined by providence for each other: they therefore separate; and as it is an established maxim, which the Portland women observe with great strictness, never to admit to plurality of lovers at one time, their honour is no-ways tarnished.   She just as soon (after the affair is declared to be broke off) gets another suitor, as if she had been left a widow, or that nothing had ever happened, but that she remained a virgin.

S: But pray, sir, did nothing particular happen upon your men coming down from London?

R: Yes, our men were much struck, and mightily pleased, with the facility of the Portland ladies; and it was not long before several of the women proved with child; but the men being called upon to marry them, this part of the lesson they were uninstructed in.   On their refusal, the Portland women arose to stone them out of the Isle; inso much that those few who did not care to take their sweethearts for better, for worse, after so fair a trial were, in reality, obliged to decamp. On this occasion, one bastard only was born; but since then matters have gone according to the ancient custom.

PORTLAND

Rabbit—the taboo word

THOUGH THERE is a general taboo against mentioning the Devil by name—topographical alternatives include Old Harry Rocks and the adjacent Old Nick's Ground in the Isle of Purbeck—it is exceedingly rare for the use of a specific 'normal' word to be banned by a community as a whole.   The one Dorset example is on Portland where islanders do not permit mention of the word 'rabbit'.

Kingsley Palmer writes in *Oral Folk Tales of Wessex*, 1973: "There is a story that the rabbits could cause a great deal of damage with their burrows, thus rendering the quarries unsafe, and had been the cause of more than one fatal accident.   While this may be partly true, the rabbit may have had some significance in pagan lore that is still partly remembered."

His latter suggestion is, however, nonsense as the rabbit was not found in Britain until its introduction by the Normans.   The similar creature of real Celtic associations is the hare but that is ground-living and hardly a hazard to the quarrymen.   As 'cony' or 'coney'—from its name in Old French—the rabbit occurs as the basis for local placenames all over Dorset.

Taboo words are, however, very much avoided in other parts of Britain.   On a television report I heard a woman describing how her daughter died of cancer in a community close to Sellafield nuclear re-processing plant, Cumbria: "It was cancer but we managed to keep that quiet for more than a year, because of the stigma."

Similarly, in northern working class cultures, one hears a string of absurd and even grotesque expressions that are invoked to avoid the use of the word "pregnant". The reluctance to admit certain words into their speech seems to extend wider than the medical field, to anything beyond a tolerable simplicity. I saw a young boy show his gran, who came from Wrexham, a new toy. "That's a nice brum-brum," she said. "It's a French car, it's a Renault," Robin explained.

"That's far too long a word for a little boy," the old lady replied.

PORTLAND/CHICKERELL

Chesil Beach bound-stone

BEATING-THE-BOUNDS ceremonies have been revived in the twentieth century as colourful anachronisms for children and the cameras but Portlanders, with their traditional disdain for mainlanders, or 'kimberlins' as they called us, never neglected their boundary. Being almost an island they have but one, on a bleak wind-swept section of Chesil Beach pebbles at the point where the East Fleet lagoon begins to widen two miles north-west from its Small Mouth entrance. From Small Mouth to here [grid reference SY 644 776] the Chesil Beach is part of the parish of Portland. It then enters the parish of Chickerell.

Bounds used to be beaten so that children would learn at an impressionable age the point beyond which they were not allowed to stray. In mainland Dorset such boundaries were generally marked by thick hedgerows that—until the post-war farming revolution of this century—had been serving the purpose since Saxon times. In the Portland case, as in featureless landscapes of other types, stones were necessary to demarcate the line.

Such things used to be taken very seriously. The commination against sinners in the sixteenth century Prayer Book includes: "Cursed is he that removeth away the mark of his neighbour's land."

Portlanders have over the ages used their energy and expertise to replace the marker stones in this inhospitable nothingness—for the practical purpose of reasserting their claim to the fishing rights and the free use of the beach for hauling ashore the shoals of mackerel. They had the job easy in 1974 when a Royal Navy helicopter of 516 Squadron dropped the new stones into position.

The Bridport News of May 1893 recorded a better attended ceremony and challenged a few of the Portlanders' assumptions:

"The Portlanders seem determined to keep up their rights, which they annually maintain by an official visit to the well-known 'bound-stone' on the Chesil Beach. Holy Thursday, or Ascension Day, is, as by custom, the day on which the ceremony takes place. This year the number attending seems to have been augmented for some reason or other; perhaps the fact of a new stone being used added importance to the affair. Be that as it may, there were many visitors, both by sea and land.

"It is said the rights of Portlanders extend to the new bound stone opposite Fleet, but the public would like to be enlightened as to the nature of those rights. There is one right at all events which does not extend beyond the Portland side of the stone, that is, we are informed that the lord of the manor of Abbotsbury, or rather the Earl of Ilchester, does not interfere with or claim the foreshore. Not that such a right would be of any use whatever, seeing the difficulty of telling where it is. The shingle shifts with the weather, and with it the foreshore, if ever such existed except in fertile imagination."

POWERSTOCK

Supernatural heat

DR. WILLIAM SYDENHAM of Wynford Eagle, near Maiden Newton, is one of Dorset's earliest recorded barrow diggers but what makes him unique is his remarkable description of supernatural heat emanating from the centre of an ancient burial mound. Whether or not you can believe it the description is clear enough but its location has been misplaced by field archaeologist Leslie Grinsell in his *Dorset Barrows* [1959]. Grinsell places it at Wynford Eagle but Sydenham's original letter about the discovery, which I transcribed for the first edition of John Aubrey's *Monumenta Britannica* [Volume Two, 1982], says the barrow was "nigh the sheephouse in the road going to Bridport".

This suggests the high sheep pastures, where isolated sheephouses were erected, on the upper downs to the south-west of Wynford Eagle. The road from Wynford Eagle to Bridport crosses the great sheep-runs at Eggardon Hill, where there are barrows which must have been prominent landmarks on the open uplands [such as that which lies in Powerstock parish at Ordnance Survey map reference SY 546 946].

Sydenham writes that he had already dug a barrow near his house—which he thought Roman, though we would now describe them as Bronze Age—but found only "black cinders like smith's coal" so he had promised a cousin from Devon that he would "try twenty more ere I found something to satisfy her curiousity."

The remainder of this description is in Sydenham's own words, in a letter of 19 November 1675 to his uncle, Dr. Thomas Sydenham [1624–89], who was in London. Only the spellings have been modernised and my amplifications are parenthesised in square brackets:

"Some of my workmen advised me to dig up the barrow in the ground, if you remember it, called Ferndown nigh the sheephouse in the road going to Bridport [the road from Wynford Eagle to Bridport crosses the sheep pastures of the higher downs at 827 feet, on Eggardon Hill] and my men offered me that if there was nothing in it they would loose their day's hire [forgo their wages], which I [a]greed to; and on they go, and on they go, and when they had cast away the earth it was full of very great flints. At length we came to a place perfectly like an oven curiously clayed round, and in the middest of it a very fair urn full of bones very firm and the urn not rotten, and black ashes a great quantity under the urn, which is like a butter-pot, made of potters' earth, but I must not omit the chiefest thing that at the first opening this oven one of my servants thrust in his hand and pulling it quickly back again, I demanding the reason of him, he told me it was very hot.

"I did also put in my hand and it was warm enough to have baked bread. Several other persons did the like, who can all testify the truth of it. This urn stood in the middle of this oven which I preserve with the bones but it is since fallen asunder, and digging further I found sixteen urns more, but not in ovens, and in the middle, one with ears [lugs] to it falling into pieces, being all full of sound bones and black ashes. I think it would puzzle the Royal Society to give a reason of the heat of the oven being fifteen hundred years old."

No one is likely to take issue with his last sentence. He then signs off: "I forebear yee farther trouble and rest, Sir, your most affectionate kinsman and humble servant."

SHAFTESBURY/MOTCOMBE [which formerly included the hamlet of ENMORE GREEN]

The byzant ceremony

IT WAS literally the case that in Shaftesbury beer was more plentiful than water. Thomas Hardy made the observation and noted that the town had a tradition of paying its water rates to the landowners at the foot of the hill. This communal ceremony verged upon a morris dance and was revived on Saturday 17 June 1972 when crowds packed the streets of the town, at the top of a 750-foot greensand plateau, to watch a procession in Elizabethan dress weave from the Guildhall and down the steep slope of Tout Hill to the springs at Enmore Green.

The custom dates back to at least the fourteenth century as in 1364, on Holy Cross Day—May 3rd, celebrating the alleged discovery by Empress Helena, the mother of Constantine the Great, of the cross on which Christ died—when the nuns of Shaftesbury Abbey transferred their dawn mass to Holy Trinity church to free themselves for the town's festivities. By 1527 it was recorded that an hour's dancing took place in the hamlet of Enmore Green—part of the tithing of Motcombe—between one o'clock and two when Katherine of Aragon, the steward of the manor of Gillingham, received through her bailiff the offerings of the townspeople for making her water available to them. The bailiff went home with a calf's head, a penny loaf, a gallon of ale and a pair of gloves. In 1655 the expensive item were the gloves at six shillings whereas the rest barely came to a florin. The beer was a shilling, the calf-head eightpence, and the bread tuppence.

The custom seems to have been transferred from 3 May to the first Sunday afterwards, no doubt to allow maximum popular participation, and in 1662 there were protests that this occasioned "some neglect of divine service" which led to it being moved to the Monday before Ascension Day [to the sixth Monday after Easter]. Sir Edward Nicholas—privy councillor, Shaftesbury mayor and lord of the manor of Gillingham—set aside the following day for a fair.

At this stage the byzant arrived, a name deriving from a Norman word for an offering rather than the besom/broom connection that is often assumed. In fact the object is most un-broomlike being an ornate mace three feet in height that weighs forty pounds and is bedecked with gold, silver and diamond embellishments. Some of these attachments were loaned for the ceremony and returned to their owners afterwards. The pageant continued until 1829 when it succumbed to the malaise of agricultural depression in the post-Napoleonic war period. This sapped the vigour of Britain's rural economies and stimulated emigrations to the industrial towns and passage overseas.

Historical pageants were in vogue in Edwardian times and the ceremony had a passing revival, again changing its date, on 12 April 1907. In 1972, after the byzant had been made roadworthy again by Bristol City Museum, the procession went the full course to the Fountain Inn where gifts of a plastic calf's head, a white loaf [no middle-class pretensions here], the gallon of ale, and a pair of white gloves were presented to local farmer Bert James.

Joe Rutter, an accountant, had carried the byzant. Traditionally it should have been followed by a newly married couple, known as the "Lord and Lady" just for the day. One would be dressed in a fair holland shirt and the other in a shirt adorned "with all the colours of the rainbow". By the early 1970s, however, marriage was going out of fashion and no couple was forthcoming.

Bert James duly gave the town's mayor, Marshall Johnson, permission for the townspeople to draw their water for another year. Shaftesbury does enjoy the attentions of the Wessex Water Board these days but the old wells survive if a little neglected with their green stone indistinguishable from the vegetation.

Water-names abound with streets such as Horseponds and Well Lane. For all that, the Enmore Green connection has subsequently been watered down though the quality of the bread did improve. When Hovis gave £10,000 to help pay for the restoration of the cobbles on Gold Hill, now associated throughout the land with their commercial and its tune, the byzant became little more than a sideshow for the top-of-town fête in June 1982. We live in flabby times and no one has since shown any inclination to keep the ceremony going.

They were a far pluckier lot in 1972. "Why are you doing all this?" I recall someone asking.

"Because they were daft enough to build a town on top of a hill without any water," was the answer she got.

SHAPWICK

The bell in White Mill Hole

THERE ARE several nineteenth century versions of a doggerel asserting that thieves stole the bell from the now-ruined church at Knowlton, near Cranborne, and dumped it in the River Stour, between Shapwick and Sturminster Marshall, when they were being pursued. The bell is credited with supernatural power that prevents its recovery from the river bed:

> *Knowlton bell is stole*
> *And thrown into White Mill Hole*
> *Where all the devils in hell*
> *Could never pull up Knowlton bell.*

White Mill is a National Trust property [Ordnance Survey map reference ST 957 006] immediately upstream from one of the most graceful mediaeval bridges in Dorset—from which the bell is said to have been cast-off.

Alternative stories state that the bell was in fact pulled up and put either into

Shapwick or Sturminster Marshall churches or taken off by a Mr. Compton of Horton.

SIXPENNY HANDLEY

Country funerals

THE GREAT WAR changed the world in a way that remains unequalled. Its effects reached all classes and every district in the county, speeded the approach of a mechanised age, and shattered attitudes and beliefs that had survived from the Middle Ages. How great this change was is shown by the memories of Frank Adams, who lived at Sixpenny Handley and was aged 84 in 1959.

Though he wrote of a world which, for him, was within living memory, there is something distant and lost about his reminiscences which cover just one of the former rules of life in the countryside—its funeral customs. And though Frank Adams wrote from a village on the edge of Cranborne Chase, the traditions he remembered were widespread in all areas.

Firstly, a little of the background to his account. One day the sexton came to him, looking scared, and saying he had dug a grave in the old part of the churchyard. He had dug into a skeleton, and was shocked to find that there were no remains of a coffin or its bits of metal. Instead was a quantity of decayed box scrub.

This burial dated from before about 1760 when coffins were an innovation in the village. Previously the bodies of the dead had been wrapped in linen though this was changed by an unpopular law that wool, for the sake of the national economy, should be used instead. The first coffins of the eighteenth century were crudely made and fitted with two handles at each side, made by the blacksmith and bent over on the inside for security. The name, date of death and the age of the deceased were formed by using stamped lead-foil letters. These were mass-produced and supplied to the undertaker—who was also the village carpenter, wheelwright and blacksmith—in sheets containing the whole alphabet and numbers up to ten. The necessary letters and numbers were cut from the sheets and tacked on the coffin lid.

Mr. Adams remembered seeing a quantity of these letters, unused odd ones, when he was a small boy early in the 1880s. The custom was that the cover of the coffin would be nailed down shortly before it was to be removed from the cottage. Before 1900, an aged undertaker had told him, the relations and others would be asked, when they had taken a last look, to go outside. The undertaker would then wrap a piece of cloth around the head of his hammer to deaden the sound when driving the nails home. When he was ready he would call the relatives back.

An hour before the funeral, Mr. Adams said, there was generally a feast when many of the neighbours would come and force a tear and ask for a *"last look on dear Martha, poor dear soul, how peaceful she do look"*. The real reason for their visit was to enjoy the "nunch" which was the local word for the meal.

At that time every cottager kept a pig or two, for a sure supply of meat during the year, and it was the practice to keep one ham in reserve for either a wedding or a funeral. The old undertaker told Mr. Adams that he had many times cut up a whole ham during one of these feasts and that often a bottle of brandy would be produced from somewhere.

Sixpenny Handley is a large country parish, with hamlets like Deanland, Woodcutts, Minchington and Gussage St Andrew, and many isolated farms and cottages. Some parts are three or four miles from the church but most had a series of tracks and footpaths that led directly to the village. Along these, Mr. Adams had often seen bearers, either four or six in number, carrying a coffin. They occasionally rested and changed over, and after the burial the mourners would return over the same route to find a tea awaiting them. On the table would be a spotless white cloth, the family's best tea service and a huge home-made cake.

On the following Sunday, the family mourners attended the first service and occupied the front pew, or two if necessary, and remained seated throughout the service. Afterwards they would walk across the churchyard and cluster around the grave to see that everything was in order.

The social problem of burying the dead eased with the formation of village benefit clubs. Most of the working class paid their shilling or two each month which helped them considerably in cases of sickness and paid a lump sum at death. At the same time, coffins became more elaborate with eight handles and plates, breastplate and ornaments, and innumerable black studs around the bottom and cover. At these funerals the coffins were draped with a pall of black or purple velvet, with a snow-white linen fringe. All that could be seen of the bearers were eight legs.

The destitute, or paupers as the poor were officially called, were provided for by the Board of Guardians. Coffins were made for the board under contract, each to the same specification, and usually cost £1 each, which included delivery. Except for two plain handles on each side, and a large breastplate the full width of the lid, there was no elaboration. The name, age and date of death were written boldly on the plate with yellow paint.

Mr. Adams said that he had been told of an occasion when one such coffin was delivered at a cottage five miles away in an adjoining parish. On arrival, the undertaker's assistant was met at the cottage by the parish nurse.

"I have brought the coffin for Mrs. . . . ., Nurse," he said. "And here my job is supposed to end, but if I can be of help in getting it up the stairs, I am willing."

"I shall be very glad," she replied, "as I have no one here to help."

After the assistant had taken the coffin into the bedroom, he removed the lid—and the nurse threw up her arms in astonishment and horror.

"What, no lining!" she said. "How perfectly disgraceful; is this all that you are allowed to do?"

The assistant answered that the board's contract had been carried out and if anything else had been added, the family would be liable for payment of the cost of the whole outfit.

"Well," said the nurse, "I am going to see her ladyship at once. Something has got to be done."

A few days later, an order came from the board that in future all parish coffins were to be lined with a material called 'Domett' and supplied with additional handles and plates on the outside. The pauperish look had gone.

Village taste in the matter of funeral furnishings was already changing. After a few years, the fashion for having everything black and sombre had given way to a brassy and gaudy phase. The villagers liked things to be showy. Even at a funeral when the hearse—the word formerly meant the framework supporting the pall—went through the village, the bearers seemed pleased to carry it. Their feelings were matched by those of the mourners who appeared equally proud to show it off.

Coffins had to be received by the village according to the rules of ancient custom. As the funeral approached, all cottage blinds would be drawn, and if a man came towards it, he would immediately stand beside the road, hat in hand, till the whole procession had passed.

One village undertaker said that at various times he had put a parcel in a coffin shortly before screwing on the lid. He told of one old man who had cut for himself, sometime before, a blackthorn stick from a hedgerow—carefully trimmed it and spent much time polishing it. This was to be his walking stick in the new world!

The old countryman also bought a new pipe and gave orders that the two articles, together with an ounce of tobacco and a full box of matches, were to be placed in the coffin beside him. His wishes were faithfully carried out.

On another occasion the undertaker prepared to place the lid on a coffin. At that moment a woman entered the room. She was the only remaining sister of the deceased and apparently the last of an old family. After placing a neat parcel by the side of her dead sister, she stood nearby and kept sight of the coffin till it was lowered in its grave: the parcel was not removed.

Church bells also played a part in the old ritual. As soon as possible after the sexton had been told of the passing of an inhabitant, the knell was tolled for half an hour. After a short pause there were three heavy clangs in quick succession if the deceased was a man; two if a woman; and one if a child. On the day of the funeral, which was usually at three in the afternoon, the bell was tolled for ten minutes, starting at two o'clock. Then at 2.30, for the remaining half-hour, it continued at minute intervals until the procession was seen approaching the lych gate.

Immediately after the service came the passing bell: it tolled for fifteen minutes and, after a brief pause, clanged out the age of the deceased with one ring for each year.

Funerals are no longer such a common part of village life. At the start of the century, the undertaker buried sixty adults and an average of a dozen children each year. By the 1950s, the average had fallen to ten adults and no children. "'Tis a long time since I buried a child," the undertaker remarked.

And a long time since the church bells clanged at a passing. Or a funeral that was not motorised. Longer still when grave goods were last slipped into the coffin, to be there when they were needed on the other side.

STINSFORD

Heedless William's Pond

A MILE east of Stinsford, on the north side of the lane that skirts the edge of the heath and leads to Tincleton, is Heedless William's Pond. This deep, oval-shaped pool is supposedly bottomless. It lies a hundred yards north-west of the

Victorian cottage that replaced the former Pond House. On the Stinsford side of this cottage, marking the parish boundary between Stinsford and Puddletown and the lands of Lord Ilchester with those of Robert Hayne, is a five feet high monolith. It is almost rounded by tooling and tapers towards the top. It is probably a Roman milestone that was removed from the course of the road across Puddletown Heath, the forest ridge to the north.

The pond [Ordnance Survey map reference SY 731 913] was probably created by gravel digging which penetrated to an underlying seam of clay. There are many other old gravel pits between Duddle Farm water-meadows and the 390 feet summit of the heath.

Heedless William is said to have been a reckless coach-and-four driver who ended his days careering off the road and into the pond on a dark night. Only his ground-ash whipstick remained above the water-line and it budded to become a tree that marks the site of his misadventure. The story clings to his pond; though there is a tendency for 'heedless' to become 'headless' in the retellings.

STUDLAND

Agglestone: with Studland Bay and the cliffs of Bournemouth beyond. The 400 ton rock is said to have fallen from the sky.

Thrown by the devil

THE BELIEF in the Isle of Purbeck was that the enigmatic Agglestone rock, a 400-ton mass of iron-impregnated sandstone which dominates Studland Heath from the top of a heather-clad hillock, was thrown by the devil from The Needles on the Isle of Wight. He was aiming at Corfe Castle but missed by four miles. The stone [Ordnance Survey map reference SZ 024 828] was formerly anvil-shaped but slipped on to its side in 1970. It is a natural relict fragment of a layer of harder stone that once covered the Bagshot Bed sands; another, the Puckstone, was associated with goblins in the popular mind and lies to the north-west.

The name Agglestone probably derives from the Old English *hagolstan*—"hailstone"—suggesting that the belief that it fell from the sky is of some antiquity and pre-dates the building of Corfe Castle to which it has since been associated.

SYMONDSBURY

Hilltop rites in a magic circle

THE SEPTEMBER harvest home celebrations in the west Dorset parish of Symonds-bury were marked by a pilgrimage to the top of a hill and the enactment of fertility rites.   The remarkable thing about their Muslim style kneeling and incantations was that the farm labourers performed them in a fashion that is redolent of the Bronze Age standing stones erected in mystic circles on the downs.   Whether the custom had that sort of antiquity is impossible to prove but it was unique in its presentation of what without any stretch of the imagination we might regard as a prehistoric ritual.

It is certainly pagan, with the single Christian adjunct being the point at which the event starts, namely the saying of grace to begin the village's traditional harvest festival imbibing of food and drink which for them and all rural settlements was traditionally the greatest communal celebration of the year.

The Bridport News recorded the custom in 1857, in a report found for me by Dr. Chris Wrigley in 1975.   In Victorian times the press and clergy were perplexed by the survival of ancient traditions and exerted pressure to substitute more restrained and praiseworthy programmes of events to replace those customary excesses that used to continue "until almost another day had dawned on an inebriated party".

This is the contemporary description of how the rituals at the Symondsbury harvest home unfolded: "Immediately after the removal of the cloth, and grace being said the whole party removed to the field to perform, what we were told, was a very ancient custom, but of which numbers of our readers uninitiated in the manners and customs of the labouring classes of their own county have perhaps never heard.

"The labourers, large and small, being arrived at an elevated spot in the middle of the field form a circle, and uncovering the head, the men bend to the ground after the manner of orientals, and rising gradually say in a solemn and we may say unearthly tone, We-e-e-e-e ha-a-a-ave-en.

"They bend again, and rise uttering the same words, then again bending, go through the same ceremony, concluding with a lusty Hurrah.   The same bendings and 'we have 'ens' are repeated thrice more when two hurrahs are given, after which three more of the solemn bendings and risings are repeated, and three loud hurrahs conclude the ceremony.

"To us this appeared a strange custom, but it is time-honoured, and undoubtedly originated from some motive with which we are unacquainted.   We must leave our honest British labourers to indulge in their 'we have 'ens' without further comment, as whatever may be its origins, it is for certain, quite harmless and inoffensive."

TRENT

The bottomless pit

THERE IS a legend at Trent, a village north-west of Sherborne, that a coach-and-horses plunged into a supposedly bottomless pit that was water-filled and disappeared without trace.   The story is associated with Trent Barrow, an uninhabited semi-wooded spot on the top of the hills a mile east of the village [Ordnance Survey map reference ST 609 187].

Primroses and shepherds' crooks

THE HEATHLAND community of Verwood was described in the nineteenth century as the "poorest place on earth". It was certainly the tough end of Dorset as far as teaching was concerned in Victorian times and the emergence of a colourful custom on Easter Monday disguised the underlying difficulties of Verwood life.

The memory that has survived is of the chapel children, and non-conformity was the norm in places of poverty, gathering behind the sixty strong Band of Hope to march around the village. The village girls wore garlands of primroses and the boys carried shepherds' crooks to which bunches of daffodils had been tied. The day ended with fruit cake for tea at the Congregational chapel.

Similarly at Whitsun there was the Club Fete on the Station Road and at Christmas the treat was an abstemious party at which all the presents on the huge fir tree came into the category of necessities. There were gloves and scarves, stockings and socks, and some books. There were never any toys. Still, such events attracted the young in an area where truancy virtually closed the schools. In September 1873 the teacher at the Anglican National School was amazed at the good attendance: "The reason I think can be assigned to the report prevalent among the children that the tea party will take place this week."

Many were from the hamlets of Eastworth, Three Legged Cross and Romford which as at Church Hill and Dewlands Common had populations as big as Verwood itself. Verwood was then still a far-flung district of Cranborne parish—as it was to remain until parochial independence in 1894—and it was the haven of the dispossessed. They came as the émigrés from the enclosure schemes elsewhere in east Dorset and in particular it attracted the new poor of the Hungry Forties, when agricultural decline caused thousands of labourers to lose their jobs and tied cottages.

There were 327 people in Verwood in 1818 and by 1841 this had risen to 684—but the 1840s saw the huge influx as by 1851 the population had reached 919.

*   *   *   *   *

Verwood offered space for homes, land for a few stock, an accessible water-table for well digging, free fuel for fires, and work for those who were desperate; for women the cottage industry was the knitting of gloves and for the men there was always the fall-back of a pocket of bog-land where they could dig clay for the thriving local potteries. The land also provided the mud for cob-walled cottages and heather for bonding, for self-built homes. A timber shuttering would rise at the rate of two feet a week, or as quick as natural drying would allow, and the building "reared" into existence. The process was known as "rearing" and the texture of the walls often shows the breaks between each week's work like the rings in a tree. Such cottages sprang up across a vast area of unclaimed waste land, covering ten square miles in all, though tending to concentrate where lane access reached the fringes of commons, and avoiding any ownership confrontations that would follow from attempts to build near the established home ranges of the ancient farms.

What riches there were in the area came through the pottery trade, and as with wool in the Cotswold, pots in Verwood is translated into visible wealth in the churchyard.   There Stephen Crutcher, a middle-man dealing in the distribution of pottery, has the most elaborate tomb.

From 1837 to 1847 the National Society for Promoting the Education of the Poor in the Principles of the Established Church established a weekday school in the parish church, with dual purpose seating that was not replaced by pews until the modernisation of the church in 1886.   A purpose-built National School, built in brick to the English Garden Wall pattern [three stretcher bricks to each header], opened on 7 October 1847 and was partitioned into two rooms for infants and older children.   An additional classroom, which rehoused the infants, was added in 1869.   A further room, to which once again the infants were removed, was built in 1899.   The school had to cope with a high proportion of what were regarded as "dull" pupils from large, rough families.

Fighting and swearing were normal, though seldom erupting into such open indiscipline as on a hot August day when two seven-year-olds stripped off their clothes during the lunch hour and began wrestling.   The year was 1867, so one hardly needs to add that Henry Sims and Herbert Haskell received a bare-bummed beating before returning to their trousers.   Caning was another custom of the times.

WEST LULWORTH/CHARMOUTH/WEYMOUTH

Napoleon's reputed visit

THERE IS a firm tradition that Napoleon landed on the Dorset coast during the period of invasion scares at the start of the nineteenth century.   Lulworth Cove is firmly linked to the story but it has also been recorded from Charmouth and Weymouth.   In the 1930s the Women's Institute at Lulworth noted their generally accepted version of the legend for the book *Dorset Up along and Down along*. The "Emperor" was seen by a young farmer's wife who spoke French and heard him sigh "Impossible" as he folded his charts and walked back towards his ship. His famous cocked hat was by no means unique to the Emperor; but on the other hand his features had been popularly available as caricatures and cartoons. So the woman might have been able to identify him.

The story is relayed with a positivism rarely heard with oral tradition: "The whole incident was watched and the conversation overheard by a local farmer's wife who had learnt French as a young girl so that she might help her father (a china merchant) in his business.   This lady was born in 1784, and lived to be 104, and was alive when the West Lulworth contributor first heard the story."

The most likely year for this visit would have been 1804 when Napoleon was emperor and personally supervising the invasion fleet being assembled at embarkation points along the eastern end of the Channel.   For eighty days he was based at Pont-de-Briques, a chateau near Boulogne, and though this period is intensely documented there are a few days when Napoleon's movements are unknown.

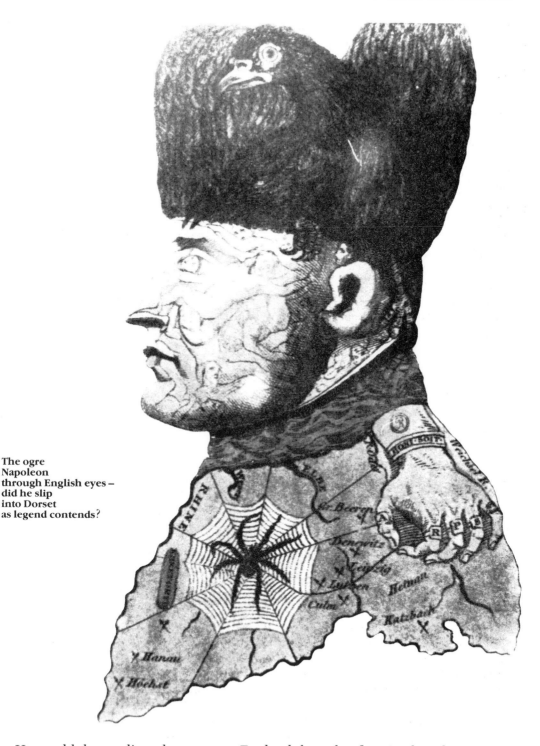

The ogre
Napoleon
through English eyes –
did he slip
into Dorset
as legend contends?

He could have slipped across to England but the fact is that despite the succession of alarms in Dorset it was Caesar's Coast—as the War Office called Kent in the summer of 1940—that was the objective of the Grande Armée. That choice would have been enforced by the tides, as David Cooper points out in issue ten of Dorset County Magazine: "The ebb out of Boulogne would take the fleet to the west but the flood tide on the English coast would then bring it back eastwards." It would also be pushed up-Channel by the prevailing south-westerly winds.

There was not, then, any prospect of invading Lulworth from Boulogne. Nearer and easier were the sandy beaches of Poole Bay not that the Grande Armée was in a position for visiting them either. Nor was French intelligence such that it needed to ascertain landing conditions on the Dorset coast; information about the English coast and its defences had been collected for centuries, and as Cooper says Napoleon approved "the sending of spies to England and of corsairs to capture English peasants and fishermen for interrogation."

Despite that I do feel it was completely in character for Napoleon to have taken a day off for the express purpose of enjoying a few steps on English soil, and Dorset may have been considered much less risky that the actual piece of coast that was the target for the two thousand craft that were being prepared to carry a hundred thousand men. There might well have been a plan for a diversionary attack to draw the English fleet down-Channel in the direction of Dorset.

Napoleon was keeping up the pressure from Brest for this express purpose, and it had an effect as George III showed in June 1804 when he told the Duke of York: "I cannot deny that I am rather hurt there is any objection made to forming so large an Army of Reserves in Dorsetshire where, or in Cornwall, I think an attack more likely than in Essex, Kent or Sussex." When the King later approved the country's anti-invasion precautions and garrisons he asked for more troops to be provided in Dorset—"for Dorset is one of the most vulnerable parts of the kingdom".

WEST PARLEY/EAST PARLEY [parish of HURN]

The Sundial on which two killers hanged in chains

VILLAGERS SAID the sundial in the churchyard at West Parley failed to keep the right time because of its grim past but that superstition was spoilt when the rector had it re-set. The two foot high hexagonal post on which the dial stands is beside the path that leads up to the porch of the twelfth century heathstone church [Ordnance Survey map reference SZ 087 968]. Its past belongs two miles to the north beside the wood which took its name, Gibbet Firs, and what was then the county boundary with Hampshire at the north-western edge of the former East Parley Common [map reference SZ 097 997] midway between its two prehistoric burial mounds.

There the bodies of Jonathan Harbin, who murdered his father, and his friend and accomplice John Gubby were hanged in chains after their execution at Winchester Gaol on 12 March 1804. Their victim, William Harbin, lived at Bounds Farm, near the River Stour at the south-east corner of Parley Green [map reference SZ 104 972]. Young Harbin had given Gubby half-a-crown to buy his participation in a vicious mugging after the old man had decided to change his will. Allegedly, the wife was also involved in the row and had encouraged her son's intervention. The attack took place on 1 December 1803 and William Harbin was clubbed unconscious.

His attackers left him for dead but though fatally injured he did not expire until the following day and it seems that he was able to name his assailants. Both were indicted by a coroner's jury at Christchurch on 6 December 1803 and Harbin was buried there, at the Priory. So began the legal process that would take the accused to the gallows at Winchester and have them returned to their parish for display in what is thought to be the last case of public gibbetting in the south of England.

Picnic parties came to the heathland knoll to see the bodies and witness the sequel of the demented Mrs. Harbin, who had now lost both her husband and her son, trying to feed the rotting corpses that were suspended from the gibbet. She threw potatoes up at their mouths and spent every day there moaning and scaring off the birds. Dr. Charles Mayo, a boy at the time, would never forget being taken from Wimborne to Parley "to see the remains of the murderers whose bones and rags swung and creaked horribly in the wind". Eventually the landowner decided that this was sufficient of both justice and sightseers and he had the gibbet sawn down. A section of the post was given to the rector of West Parley and someone had the bright idea of turning it into a sundial.

WHITCHURCH CANONICORUM/CHIDEOCK/DORCHESTER

Curse that still bites

THE CURSE on lands sequestrated or filched from persecuted Roman Catholics in west Dorset's Marshwood Vale is still remembered, if not with dread, in the pasture lands and far-flung settlements of the parish of Whitchurch Canonicorum. This is Dorset's backwoods country and to understand the strength of the shudders that rippled on into legend and superstition it is necessary to go through the unpalatable process of summarising the judicial barbarity that left such burdens of guilt with the host community.

The events unfolded around a Roman Catholic enclave centred upon Chideock Castle, now a grassy earthwork on the north side of the village [Ordnance Survey map reference SY 423 930], which was owned by the Arundell family and had its resident chaplain. What they did in private did not offend the sensibilities of the general population in the Marshwood Vale but their very existence outraged the puritans in the county town of Dorchester and they were the bigots with power on their side as they provided the juries for the region's assize court. The excesses they would perpetrate are horrific; the more so because they were carried out in the name of the law and God.

Father Thomas Pilchard from Chideock was executed at Dorchester, at Gallows Hill which was at the south end of the present Icen Way, on 21 March 1587. For being a member of an outlawed religion he suffered the traitor's death of half-hanging, being cut down alive, disembowelled whilst still conscious and then quartered. First they dragged him on a hurdle so roughly that he arrived at the gallows from the gaol—then at the High Street end of Icen Way which was called Gaol Lane—in a state already approaching death. What followed, however, tended to revive him as instead of hanging for a reasonable interval he was cut down at the moment of being strung up. He then dropped not into a heap but on to his feet and faced his executioner who "either struck with fear or through some supernatural agency" rushed at his victim in a frenzy and "plunged the knife in his belly and left it there".

Naked and wounded, the priest turned to the officers of the court and asked: "Mr Sheriff, is this your justice?"

This provoked the executioner into utter rage and he tore the priest's bowels from his belly and cut the quarters of his body for display on the town walls: "Dorchester and the whole surrounding country was stricken with terrible storms, and terrified with such horrible and unusual lightnings until the limbs were removed and the like had never been heard of." Contemporary evidence is quoted in *Chideock and its Martyrs*, a book published in 1926, to show that others died with Father Thomas, some of whom he had converted, and that there were appalling consequences for the instigators of his martyrdom: "All who took part in his death met with a speedy retribution. The executioner and the greater part of the jury came to a bad end almost immediately. The Sheriff from being a rich and powerful man died miserably within two years, having fallen into great adversity. The keeper of the prison fell sick immediately, and conferred to those around him that the devils were striving for him and they would presently have him; but he saw Mr. Pilchard standing with a cross betwixt them and him."

Father Thomas was the first of many Chideock martyrs. On 4 July 1594, again at Dorchester's Gallows Hill, Father John Cornelius of the Society of Jesus was executed along with Thomas Bosgrove, John Carey and Patrick Salmon who were servants in the Arundell household. John Cornelius had gained a reputation as an exorcist. After the ritual mutilations his head was fixed to the top of the gallows where it was seen by Miss Arundell who claimed it was encircled by a bright halo. It is said to have been removed because the town started to experience calamities, and the severe visitation of plague the following year would be attributed to his execution.

* * * * *

The most unexpected of the Chideock martyrdoms came to Father Hugh Green at the beginning of the English Civil War. In February 1642 he was innocently following a royal proclamation that ordered all Catholic priests to leave the realm. Father Hugh hurriedly packed his bags and was doing just that, being in the process of boarding a ship to France from Lyme Regis, when he was arrested. He was told that the proclamation had expired the previous day. From Lyme he followed the same route to Dorchester, its gaol, England's law, and a staunch puritan jury. His execution and disembowelment on 19 August 1642 was in slow motion and took half an hour to complete, to the general delight of an exceedingly hostile crowd who were enjoying their first blood of the war. The news was still fresh that Charles I had sent his cavaliers to act against the puritan Parliament at York.

Chideock Castle would itself be a victim of the country's split. It fell to the Parliamentary army and was demolished in 1645. This time its priest hid in the woods of Marshwood Vale, still largely a forest rather than a land of little dairies, and avoided capture.

A number of local Roman Catholics were penalised, including William Warren [or Wareham] of Whitchurch Canonicorum. The faith was maintained, however, in these outlying parts and another member of the Whitchurch family, Father John Wareham, was the priest to the Catholic community in the Chideock area at the end of the seventeenth century. It was perhaps these few safeguards that these people had against the excesses of the majority that a general belief gained ground that those who took lands from ousted or persecuted Catholics would suffer a curse that rendered the ground useless and themselves afflicted with disease and grief.

Sylvia Creed, writing *Dorset's Western Vale* which I published in 1987, came across a Whitchurch Canonicorum victim of a virulent soil disease which in past-times would have been immediately ascribed to the curse: "The story goes that a farmer in the Vale gave the game away regarding the infiltration of these Roman Catholics into the area. Retribution was fast in that his farmland was 'cursed' by the Catholics and it is said that soil on this particular farm is unproductive and difficult to cultivate. Apparently there has been some fairly recent 'proof' of this curse. A resident of Whitchurch, whilst dismantling an obsolete electricity pylon happened to get some clay from this farm on his hands. Within a very short time his hands had become infected and swollen. A local doctor advised him that he had picked up 'swine fever' from 'mucking about' in this part of the Marshwood Vale, and that it would take three years to clear up. By all accounts it was the acidity in this soil that caused the malady, and the doctor had seen it happen before."

It is a land that seems abnormally afflicted with unusual farming accidents. David Popham, writing on "The Vale where nobody goes" in the Dorset County Magazine in 1969—that title could never be used since—mentions that "only a few years ago a man digging a well died in the clay's oily fumes." One inexplicable and tragic moment of forgetfulness came when a young farm worker electrocuted himself by raising a pipe until it touched 400,000 volts in the wires of the great 160-feet pylons that stride across the Marshwood Vale and which he had grown up and worked with every day.

WHITCHURCH CANONICORUM/STANTON ST. GABRIEL

Saint for sore eyes

THOMAS GERARD wrote the first book solely about Dorset, *A Survey of Dorsetshire*, in the 1620s, though its was not published until 1732 when its authorship was wrongly attributed to John Coker. In it Gerard mentions the *"Mershwood* [Marshwood] *Vale* in the heart or midest wherof lieth *Whitechurch* [Whitchurch Canonicorm] the now chiefe Towne, which took Name from one St. *White* a Virgin Martyr, whose Well the Inhabitants will shewe you not farre off in the Side of an Hill, where she lived in Prayer and Contemplation, unto whose Honour a Church beeing built was from her named *Whitechurch*; and, that you may not

think they feigne all this, you shall finde her registred in your ordinarie Alma-
nack, the third Day of October, by the Name of St. *Candida* [the latinisation of
'White'].''

In this extract I preserve the original spellings apart from modernising its use
of the long-s [f] into a standard-s. The sacred well that Gerard describes lies
near the northern edge of the parish of Stanton St. Gabriel on the south-west side
of Morcombelake, on the west side of the track about 130 yards south from Ship
Farm [Ordnance Survey map reference SY 399 937]. It is just below the east
slope of Chardown Hill and is known as "Saint Vita's Well" in the local dialect.
There is an immense amount of local folklore. The periwinkles on the hill
above, which merges with the larger Stonebarrow Hill, are called "Saint
Candida's Eyes" and the well is a traditional "sovereign cure for sore eyes"
provided that they are immersed at first-light. Bent pins were offered to the
water as token sacrifice, and there was a set recitation: "Holy well, holy well,
take my gift and cast a spell."

As for the saint, she was not "White" at all but "Wite". Despite this the
popular mind associates her with the colour as firmly as ever. The white line
that divides the tides on a flat sea is known in west Dorset as "Saint W[h]ite's
Trail". Similarly, the Breton fishermen call it "Saint Blanche's Causeway" and
there is a legend of English pirates abducting a religious girl from St. Cast, called
Blanche, who walked back home across the water. "God calls me back to
Brittany," she explained. Later she was said to have repeated the act to un-nerve
another wave of troublesome English. This side of the Channel she was called
Gwen. It is said that she went on to have seven children and that they all
eventually became bishops and saints; even a stolen statue of Saint Blanche,
carried off by English raiders, was credited with the power of walking on water.

If Saints Blanche/Wite/White/Candida are synonymous then that quality
would help the explanation of how she came to Whitchurch. Sylvia Creed
attempts this in *Dorset's Western Vale*, 1987: "The Norsemen conquered Brittany
in 914 and occupied it until 939. This was a great disaster for the area and
resulted in an influx of Breton refugees into the West of England. During this
evacuation they brought the relics of their saints with them and one supposes
that the bones of St. Wite were amongst them, and were laid to rest at Whitchurch." Fifty years later, King Alfred would have had the original wooden
chapel replaced with a stone church, that has evolved into the present building.

*   *   *   *   *

The enduring local legend, however, is that she was a Saxon hermitess slaugh-
tered by Danish pirates in a raid upon Charmouth. This is said to have happened
in 831 and involved a force of 15,000 but I have yet to be shown contemporary
documentary evidence. Likewise I am unconvinced by the favourite academic
version, their flavour of the month, which has Saint Wite as one of the victims of
the mass-martyrdom that ended Boniface's attempt to convert the Germans in
775. Its weakness is that it leaves a lot of bones a long way from home.
Boniface's remains were carried to Fulda but it seems unlikely for a logistical
means to have existed for the bringing home of his acolytes. Even in the
conflicts of the highly mechanised twentieth century it was highly unusual for
the English dead to be shipped back from the continent.

For all that, Whitchurch Canonicorum is the only church in England, other
than Westminster Abbey, that retains the original shrine and relics of the saint to
whom it is dedicated. Saint Wite has an early thirteenth century shrine with

three oval openings which are perpetually stuffed with cards and letters begging her intercession on behalf of the sick.   Above is a stone coffin with a top of Purbeck marble.   The somewhat decayed cross on top does not belong here but was placed there in 1890 when it was removed from the chancel gable.

Inside the coffin is a leaden reliquary, measuring 2 feet 5 inches, with the inscription "+hIC.REQUESCT.RELIQE.SCE.WITE" [Here lie the relics of Saint Wite].   The contents were examined in 1900 after the tomb had been split by subsidence.   They had been opened before, probably in the sixteenth century, and on top was a single thigh-bone, fourteen inches long.   This substantiated a local tradition that one of the thigh-bones was missing and by an amazing coincidence it was about to turn up in London; relics found in Lambeth Palace around 1910 included one labelled "the thigh bone of Saint Candida" [her Latin name]. The custom when an archbishop translated a saint's bones was for him to take one away as a memento.

Culliford Tree, in the parish of Whitcombe, is reputedly the Music Barrow.

WHITCOMBE

The Music Barrow

ONE OF the nicest Dorset beliefs was that a sweet melody could be heard from the Music Barrow at Culliford Tree, to the east of Came Wood [Ordnance Survey map reference SY 699 855], on the crest of the downs between Sutton Poyntz and Broadmayne.   There is a multitude of Bronze Age burial mounds around the one that supports the beech clump known as Culliford Tree.

The tradition, recorded by the antiquarian Charles Warne in his *Celtic Tumuli of Dorset*, 1868, clearly attaches to a specific mound but which is by no means clear.   It requires the prospective listener to lay his ear to the ground close to the apex at midday.

I have happened to be on Culliford Tree at noon Greenwich Mean Time—noon by the sun, as I cannot imagine a spirit tuning to European Summer Time—but it was silent.

The absence of sound I put down to the damage that Warne and his barrow digging contemporaries inflicted upon the centres of these mounds.   I wish too that earth spirits could protect the surviving antiquities.   What is needed is a curse that whosoever ploughs an ancient monument shall not live to bank another subsidy cheque.

There must be something special about Culliford Tree.   Out of all the barrows hereabouts it was chosen by the Saxons for the meeting place of a hundred-court. Excavation in 1858, which left the depression in the top, revealed four secondary burials and a cremation.

The prediction

ANTHONY ETTRICKE of Holt Lodge, north of Wimborne, was sure he would die in 1691—which is a magical date as it reads the same upside down. He was born in 1622, on a Sunday as John Aubrey recorded: "His mother would say he was a Sundaye's Bird." That's the other clue to his obsession: he would in 1691 be 69-years-old—and that also reads the same either way up.

In the event he saw out 1691 and we might know none of it but for the fact he had it carved on his wooden coffin set in the wall of Holy Trinity chapel at Wimborne Minster. When he was finally put there a half-hearted attempt was made to change the date into the unmagical 1703.

The empty Ettricke tomb at Wimborne Minster – set to be neither inside nor outside the church – with its magical 1691 half-heartedly converted into a prosaic 1703.

The other odd thing is that the coffin lies in a recess in the wall, because he was said to have left instructions that ruled out anywhere else: "When I die I do not want to be buried below ground, above ground, inside the Minster, or outside the Minster."

John Hutchins exaggerated when he said of Anthony Ettricke that he was "very humoursome, phlegmatic and credulous". Ettricke, a reader at the Middle Temple, was an observer at a witch trial and expressed scepticism about the evidence and its presentation. Aubrey was quite prepared to believe in all sort of supernatural signs but Ettricke, he notes, would not go that far: "In the time of King Charles II, the Drumming at the House of Mr Monpesson of Tidworth made a great Talke over England. They did have some times Knockings: and if they sayd: Devill, knock so many knocks: so many knocks would be answered: But Mr Ettricke some times whispered the words: and it was then no returne." Ettricke fooled about with the supernatural. He had whilst at Magdalen Hall, Oxford, frightened a freshman with conjuring, causing the learned old Dr. Ralph Kettell to say of the perpetrator—Ettricke was a very short man—that on the following Tuesday he would "conjure up a Jackanapes to be his Great-grandfather".

John Aubrey's *Brief Lives* is packed with trivial gossip and Anthony Ettricke makes his appearances but there is none of the transparent loopiness which Hutchins implies and which Aubrey would have delighted in recording. Instead they nearly drowned together, at the time of the Restoration, when returning from a month in Ireland they "were like to be ship-wrakt at Holyhead, but no hurt donne".

Ettricke's place in history came on the morning of Wednesday 8 July 1685 when a ragged figure dragged from a ditch in the parish of Woodlands on the west side of Horton Common was identified as James, Duke of Monmouth, self-proclaimed King of England. Ettricke was the closest magistrate. He started the committal proceedings at Holt Lodge and sent Monmouth on his way to Ringwood and the Tower of London where he would lose his head.

The third tradition about Ettricke at Wimborne is that his coffin is in fact empty as he was buried in a vault below. This statement, first recorded in 1750 by the traveller Dr. Richard Pococke, was proved during the minster's restoration programme of 1855–57. There, below the coffin, the builders found his remains—still in a moist state—and returned them to the same place when they had finished working on the wall.

WIMBORNE ST GILES

The Remedy Oak
at King's Wood,
in the parish of
Wimborne St. Giles,
where a king is
said to have given
a royal cure.

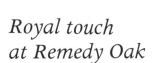

*Royal touch
at Remedy Oak*

THERE IS a plate on the Remedy Oak, by the roadside in a wooded tract of country where the eastern heathlands give way to the chalky foothills of Cranborne Chase, that records its legend: "According to tradition, King Edward VI sat beneath this tree and touched for the King's Evil, circa 1552." The disease was scrofula, a tuberculosis of the lymph glands which caused painful and unsightly swellings, and it was believed to be cured by a king's touch. By the mid-seventeenth century such beliefs were institutionalised and in 1684 John Browne, "Chirurgeon in ordinary to his Majesty," published *Charisma Basilicon, or, The Royal Gift of Healing Strumaes or King's Evil* in which he showed from registers kept by members of the royal household that 92,000 had been touched for the disease between 1660 and 1682.

The Remedy Oak preserves the memory of an unfortunate person who begged the royal touch when the king passed through Dorset. To find the tree you take the B3081 between Verwood and Cranborne. A mile from Verwood you look out for Sutton Holms which is a farmstead in dense woodland. Half a mile west from here there is an isolated cottage known as Remedy Gate, at the turning to Woodlands, opposite Sutton Common.

Remedy Oak stands a few yards along the Woodlands turn, beside the verge on the east side of the lane opposite the cottage gate. It is in the parish of Wimborne St Giles [Ordnance Survey map reference, to eight figures, being SU 0513 1001 not that they even bother to mark it on their 6-inch map]. The tree, which has a massive hollow trunk, is part of the King's Wood. It still supports a healthy crown and a heavy crop of acorns.

WOODSFORD

Woodsford Castle: tradition asserts it has a bigger thatched roof than any other house.

The biggest in Britain?

WOODSFORD CASTLE is not only unusual in having made the transformation from castle to flat dwellings but it has picked up a castle-sized thatched roof along the way. This has led to a local tradition that its 330 square yards of wheat straw is the largest area of thatch of any inhabited building in the country. Overall, however, it must lose out in the non-inhabited category to a few of the exceedingly long tithe barns. Until one of these is chosen for a barn conversion then Woodsford lays claim to the title of the biggest thatched house in the British Isles.

Woodsford Castle is on the south side of the River Frome [Ordnance Survey map reference SY 756 903] near Sturt's Weir Hatches, four miles east of Dorchester. Beside it in the fields are the traces of a moat and it was indeed once a genuine castle, the south half being a fortified house built by the Belett family about 1300. The northern half was added by the de Bryans fifty years later.

The castle was "besieged and beaten down with Ordnance" in either 1460 or 1540, and by 1625 was "now almost ruinated". Soon after this its fortunes changed and it was transformed into a rustic three-storey country house by the Strangways, the Earls of Ilchester. Mediaeval touches were retained. The bathroom used to be the chapel and there is a fine piscina of the 'decorated' period, with a pointed head. The chimney arch in the kitchen, of two huge curving stones and a tiny keystone, surmounts a great open fireplace that is fourteen feet wide.

There were five towers, of which the north-east survives. It still has its archery slits which command the east wall and the entrance to the kitchens.

Index to the section on
Legends and Customs, pages 98 to 138